GEOFF
HAMILTON
A MAN AND HIS GARDEN

GEOFF HAMILTON

A MAN AND HIS GARDEN

A PORTRAIT OF BRITAIN'S
BEST-LOVED GARDENER

GAY SEARCH
WITH
TONY HAMILTON

Published by BBC Worldwide Ltd,
80 Wood Lane, London W12 OTT

First published 1998
Reprinted 1998 (twice)
First published in paperback 2000
Text © Gay Search 1998
Introduction and Last Word © Tony Hamilton 1998

The moral right of the authors has been asserted

ISBN 0 563 38465 4 (hardback)
ISBN 0 563 55154 2 (paperback)

Commissioning editor: Nicky Copeland
Copy editor: Hugh Morgan
Project editor: Martha Caute
Art director: Ellen Wheeler
Designer: Harry Green
Picture researcher: Susannah Playfair

Set in Bembo and Trajan
Printed and bound in Great Britain by
Butler and Tanner Ltd, Frome & London
Colour separations by Radstock Reproductions Ltd,
Midsomer Norton
Jacket and colour sections printed by
Laurence Allen Ltd, Weston-super-Mare

CREDITS

BBC Worldwide would like to thank the following for providing photographs:
Between pages 32–3:
David Hislop page 3b;
Monica Meeneghan page 8.

Between pages 96–7:
BBC *Gardeners' World Magazine*/Stephen Hamilton page 4bl and 4br; Stephen Hamilton pages 5b and 6; *Radio Times/* Warwick Bedford page 8.

Between pages 160–1: Stephen Hamilton pages 1, 2, 3tl, 5 and 7b; Robert Rathbone page 3tr; Clay Perry page 4t; Lu Jeffery page 4br; *Farmers' Weekly* Picture Library page 6t; *Rutland Times/* Rod Crowther page 6b; David Austin Roses page 7t.

All other photographs courtesy the Hamilton family.

The verse from Hilaire Belloc's poem 'Duncton Hill', from *Complete Verse*, published by Random House UK Ltd, is reprinted by permission of the Peters Fraser and Dunlop Group Ltd.
© The Estate of Hilaire Belloc 1970.

CONTENTS

INTRODUCTION
BY TONY HAMILTON

It isn't given to many people to be born one of identical twins. (You can check that with the Office for National Statistics if you like. I think you'll find it is not an extravagant claim!) So most people never know what it's like to have your own Department of Social Security, your own marriage guidance counsellor, your own version of Ken Dodd or Tommy Cooper, somebody permanent to set the world to rights with and somebody just to beat about the ears when life is too much.

But even if you were lucky enough to have been given that birthright, it would be rare indeed if you were given a brother as extraordinary as mine.

Geoff was firstly a man with an enormous generosity of spirit. He had that rare ability to engender genuine love among the people he met because he showed a deeply held respect and regard for their feelings and their views. He was also, in spite of his enormous popular acclaim, the very last person to even notice it. As a show biz personality Geoff made a very good country bumpkin. I don't think he knew himself how popular he was, even to the day he died. Yet I used to get a multitude of compliments and affectionate remarks about him, which perhaps people were too reticent to make direct to him.

He was also amazingly generous with his money – even in the days when he didn't have any. Talking to me one day, he asked me how my business was going. Well, we were having some recession problems at the time, so I told him I was a bit worried about the future. 'For goodness' sake,' he said, 'you don't have to worry. After all, it's only money. How much do you need to put you right?'

Well, I didn't want to borrow from Geoff, so I said (very tongue in cheek), 'Well, a hundred thousand pounds should do it' – knowing he didn't have that kind of money. 'I'll give you a hundred thousand,' he said – and he meant it! He would have scraped up the money from somewhere, and he would have given it to me. Not lent it, given it. And I know he would never have mentioned it ever again. Some man! (Needless to say, I didn't accept his offer, but I never forgot it was there.)

He also overpaid his staff outrageously, gave them extravagant bonuses, helped them buy their houses, and even helped one of them to start his own business. He loved the idea that his efforts were securing a good living for them, and he did everything in his power to ensure that security was what they felt.

Geoff's second giant talent was his sense of humour. Nobody could ever be glum when Geoff was about. He was a rogue and a maverick, and everybody who worked with him delighted in it. I feel sure that if the BBC had known how much time was spent with the film crew rolling around the floor in helpless laughter, a mandarin with a clipboard would have been down to put things right. I've met a number of the people who worked with Geoff and, without exception, they all say what enormous fun it was. You will read in the book about some of the things he (and occasionally I) got up to, and I have to assure you that they are all true.

Geoff was always a very creative man, who could dream up ingenious ideas that would fit the smallest garden. He was a genuine man of the people, with a passionate belief in what he was doing and an earnest desire to share it with his viewers. So he had a guiding principle in all he did. Make it accessible to the man or woman stuck with 50 square yards of heavy clay and builders' rubble in a modest council house in Barnsley or Basingstoke or even Billingsgate. Geoff was a man who got his hands dirty because he wanted to show how to get results, not just to tour stately homes or show exotic plants with funny names, although he never underestimated the value of the ideas that could be generated by such things – as long as they could be translated into something that all his viewers, rich, poor, disabled, young or old, could do as soon as the programme was over. So he didn't appear in a suit and tie (in fact he was once voted the worst-dressed man on television); he got his hands in the soil, his wellies in his pond and his heart in his work for the people he served.

Geoff was also well aware that he didn't know it all and occasionally got things wrong. But the unusual thing about him was that he believed he should share with his viewers his mistakes as well as his successes. This put him firmly in touch with them because they knew that they were not watching somebody whose expertise they couldn't aspire to.

But the thing that I probably admired most about Geoff was his tireless efforts to ensure that the environment, which he had grown to love so passionately, was not ravaged by people simply out to make a fast buck. So he fought savagely against the vandals who were destroying majestic limestone pavements, and in fact, as a result of money donated after his death, Plantlife, one of his favourite conservation organizations, was able to buy Winskill Stones – a huge limestone pavement in Yorkshire.

He also campaigned against the use of peat – the extraction of which was (and sadly still is) destroying our last remaining peat bogs and wetlands – encouraging gardeners to use a perfectly good substitute: coir. His efforts did sharpen his viewers' appreciation of the iniquity of using peat and also boosted the sale of coir, which kept a good few Sri Lankans off the breadline into the bargain. No television commentator, gardener or otherwise, has ever presented the case for a sane approach to the use of our natural resources so well and so powerfully – and I wonder if anyone ever will. Geoff is a hard act to follow.

Because we were identical, I shared a vicarious celebrity with Geoff, often being mistaken for him, and I was pretty proud of what the old boy had achieved. People would approach me in pubs, or at parties or in factories and say, 'Do you mind if I ask you a personal question?' – and my reply would always be 'Yes, I am!' Then there would follow either a glowing tribute to Geoff or a gardening question. I did my best to answer, but I'm sure there are some people who now regret they asked.

Geoff was a wonderful man. He was a good writer, a good presenter, he was a good gardener, but most of all, believe me, he was a good man. He lived for his garden, his family, his viewers, his readers and his colleagues. He died on a charity cycle ride for Sustrans (the organization which is working to promote a National Cycle Network in the UK, as well as designing and building new cycle routes), trying to help others to improve the world we live in.

Many people have asked me if I still grieve for him – and the answer is no. We had built up such a strong bond between us that nothing could break it. Of course, I miss the old devil like crazy. I just long for him to walk through my front door with Lynda, like he used to, plonk himself into a chair and start telling Carol and me about all the funny, crazy, wonderful things that had happened to him. I know he won't, but I also know that he lived the lives of ten men. And he was my brother!

May I also take this opportunity to thank all the people who contributed to this book, for sparing their time and their thoughts to remember an old friend. Most of all I must thank Gay Search for the incredible research work she did, turning up people I thought were lost for ever, for being so very kind and sensitive about the feelings of all the family and just for being so very good to work with.

CHAPTER ONE

BOY

For the man who was to become the nation's most popular gardener, a two-up, two-down in Tollet Street, just off the Mile End Road in London's East End, was a rather unlikely birthplace. Geoffrey Stephen Hamilton was born on 15 August 1936, three years after his older brother, Barry Mark, and thirty-five minutes before his identical twin, Anthony George – the thirty-five minutes, as Tony says with a wry smile, that shaped the whole course of their lives. 'If you're the older one when you're a kid, it gives you one great asset – it gives you power.'

Geoff subtly but unstintingly exerted his dominance over Tony right up until the day he died. The earliest memory Tony has of Geoff is of them lying together in the big double pram in the hallway where they were put to sleep for part of the day, and Geoff sitting up, grabbing his brother's hair, pulling a chunk out, waving it around and shouting gleefully, 'Dot sum!'

Geoff was always more stubborn and strong-minded than Tony, who became the diplomat of the family, the peacemaker. If they'd ever done something seriously wrong, he was the one who was sent to explain it to their parents because he was the youngest and the most vulnerable looking. Tony recalls that Geoff was much more inventive and creative than he was too. In comparison with him, Tony was more thoughtful and methodical, but he didn't have the flair and panache that Geoff always had. 'All his life,' Tony says, 'Geoff surprised me with his ideas and views about politics, religion, business, the environment, and so on, which was very stimulating to live with.' A small but significant verification of this came up while they were going through their mother's effects after she died in 1996. It was a letter from Barbara Kellett, their violin teacher at the Hertfordshire Rural Music School, and it was dated 15 April 1947:

> *Dear Mrs Hamilton,*
>
> *You will be glad to know that both twins passed the Grade One violin exam. Tony with 116 and Geoffrey with 114. The pass mark is 100. I hope that they will continue to make as much progress as they have this term. It is the practising which is so important.*
>
> *I find Geoffrey the more musical of the two,* though the hard work of this term (and would they have been so keen, if it hadn't been for the exam?!) has brought them level in their playing.*
>
> *With best wishes,*
> *Yours sincerely,*
> *Barbara Kellett*
>
> ** Please don't mention this to them*

'Of course, what Miss Kellett didn't realize was that she was the most beautiful violin teacher who ever taught two impressionable eleven-year-old boys, and we were both deeply in love with her. The violin playing was actually excruciating. Even the dog used to run to the bottom of the garden when we began our famous "Bluebells of Scotland" duet.'

Geoff and Tony were always known as 'the twins' or 'the boys' and their mother used to dress them identically, so Geoff felt in their early years that they were very much an exhibit. 'People would say, "Oh, look at them. Aren't they alike? Aren't they lovely? Come and have a look."'

Even so, Geoff felt that the advantages of being identical twins far outweighed the disadvantages. 'Very early on I realized that Tone and I had something special – we had each other. There were rivalries, of course, but nothing ever got out of hand. The strange thing is that in my life I've never found two people more stimulating to talk to than my two brothers. It used to annoy our wives at family gatherings. In no time the three of us would be off in a corner, talking, arguing, discussing, singing, composing limericks, forgetting the rest of the world.'

Tony agrees. 'It was a real privilege, being twins. For a start you have built-in support systems, and second there is always someone to have fun with, someone who is exactly the same age, has exactly the same genes, and so shares the same interests.' And as Geoff pointed out, no one picked on you at school because there were two of you, or, in their case, three of you because Mark was around too.

Both Geoff and Tony in later life felt their arrival must have been very tough on Mark (he adopted 'Mark', his grandfather's second name, in preference to 'Barry' in his twenties) because not only did they become the apple of their mother's eye and the centre of attention, but when they were older they were so involved with each other that they weren't even much use to him as playmates. 'I was told that one day when we were all out together,' said Mark, 'a neighbour saw the twins in their double pram and said, "Oh, aren't they lovely? They're so lovely!" When she'd gone, I said to my mother, "Aren't I lovely too, Mum?" I don't remember that, of course, and I honestly don't remember resenting them. We had our battles, of course, as all kids do, but most of the time I loved them madly, and I certainly used to stick up for them. I remember one time when I must have been nine or ten and they were being attacked by the Harvey brothers from down the road. I saw a large disc made of plywood, which belonged to our lodger, advertising his business and which he used to bolt to the spare wheel on the back of his car. I picked this disc up, skimmed it at them, and caught John Harvey in the neck. How it didn't take his head off I will never know. Of course, they fled, and never attacked Geoff and Tony again.'

Mark, who now lives in Majorca, where he works as a photographer, believes that Geoff's position in the family – in the middle – had a considerable bearing on his personality. 'Tony, the youngest, is the most responsible and the most caring of the three of us. He was the one who was always there for our mother when she needed help. I am unequivocally the black sheep of the family, the "alternative" one, a professional musician and ex-commercial photographer who dropped out, and Geoff was the one in the middle. Geoff was caring and responsible too, but not as much as Tony. Geoff was a bit alternative, but not as much as me. Geoff said to me, only about five years ago, "What really annoys me about you, Mark, is that you got to be the black sheep and I always wanted that role." He was joking, but I'm sure there was an element of truth in it.'

Their parents, Cyril and Rosa Hamilton, were both East Enders. Cyril's father was a fishmonger and family legend has it that Cyril started work selling newspapers on the street at four years old – except on Thursdays, when his trousers went in the wash. He clearly showed a genuine talent for selling, because when he left school at 14 he started selling coal door to door – 'on the knocker' – and over the years he built up a very successful business, eventually selling engineering parts to industry. He took enormous pride in the fact that he was the only man to sell rubber to the Dunlop Rubber Company, and that once, having sold some parts to the chief maintenance engineer of a factory, he inadvertently went to the back door of the same factory and managed to sell another lot of parts to the assistant maintenance engineer. On another occasion, when he was selling sheets of gasket material, he turned up at a factory and went into his patter. The man stopped him mid-flow and said, 'Come with me,' leading him through the factory to the stores. 'See these stores?'

he said. 'Last time you were here you sold me enough of this stuff to last 200 years, so I've used it to *build* the stores!' He was the most resourceful and enterprising of men, with a strong sense of being the family provider. Tony recalls a childhood holiday in Wales when Rosie told Cyril that they were running a bit short of cash. 'You go off to the beach with the boys,' he said, 'and I'll go and sell something.' And he came back with a big smile, a fistful of cash and some exciting ideas about what to do with the rest of the holiday.

As well as being a gifted salesman, he was also a very funny man, with a dry, offbeat sense of humour that he passed on to his sons. Tony tells the story about going to meet him from work at Broxbourne aerodrome one very cold day when he and Geoff were about seven. 'He was cycling home on his big sit-up-and-beg bicycle with one hand on the handlebars and the other hand behind his back. I now know that he was doing it because he only had one glove, because gloves – or "pashas", as we called them (after 'Glubb Pasha', a British soldier in the Middle East at that time) – were very hard to come by during the war and so it was a way of keeping the other hand a bit warmer until he could swap them over. But we were puzzled by this, and Geoff, ever the bold one, asked him why he was riding like that. "Son," he said gravely, "never let your right hand know what your left hand is doing!" And he then pedalled off, leaving us standing there wondering what he meant. I was about 20 when the penny finally dropped. The old devil wasn't just having a joke with us, it was really a joke for himself.' Tony also has a photograph of him in his greenhouse with Geoff, holding up a pot and pointing at it, but if you look closely you see that he's got a cigarette sticking out of his ear!

Cyril was also very intelligent and, lacking a proper education, educated himself, mainly at the Highgate Library. He became a very political man. In his youth he had been a Communist, then became a committed Socialist and taught politics at the Workers' Educational

Association. By the end of his life, though, he had become a Conservative, a Mason and, through his Masonic work, a Freeman of the City of London. Geoff and Tony used to have long political arguments with him, sometimes until 3 or 4 o'clock in the morning, right up until he died in 1981. Tony believes that it was largely from his father that Geoff got his compassionate view about people and his desire to help them get what they deserved out of life.

Cyril was a very practical man, good with his hands, especially in carpentry, and he was also a keen gardener, both qualities he passed on to the twins. Geoff adored Cyril and admired him greatly, and throughout his life he often used to quote him – 'As my old dad used to say.'

If Geoff's practicality, humour, intellectual curiosity and political views came from his father, then his talent as a performer – and it takes real talent to appear *not* to be performing as successfully as Geoff did – came from Rosa's side of the family. Her father, Alfred Mark Abrahams, was a successful music-hall singer touring the country, from the Finsbury Park Empire all the way to the Glasgow Empire, where, he used to say, he always got the bird. But then everybody got the bird at the Glasgow Empire, so it didn't worry him. He used to work with two songs – one to sing and one up his sleeve in case he got an encore. His stage name was Alf Davis – he was Jewish, and it was thought then that you couldn't succeed in show business with an obviously Jewish name. These days, as Geoff once pointed out, any family would be delighted for their daughter to marry a pop star, but at that time show business was not considered respectable. So in order to marry Harriet, Rosa's mother, Alf had to give up the stage.

One day Harriet, while packing for Alf to go away, discovered pictures of chorus girls in his suitcase – not scantily clad, because they weren't in those days – and said to him, 'You're not going to mix with these sort of people! This is your last tour, and when you come back you'll have to do something else.' While he was away she saved all her money – she worked as a forewoman in an aircraft factory, putting the canvas on the wings of wooden aeroplanes – and, when he came back from touring, a London taxi that she had bought for him was standing outside the door. 'Right,' said Harriet, resolute to the core, 'you've got a bicycle, so now you do the Knowledge and get your badge.' For six months, while he did exactly that, she supported them both, and he became a taxi driver for the rest of his life.

During the First World War he was called up and became a train driver in France. He told Tony that one day he found that he'd driven his train behind enemy lines, and he could see Germans on either side of the track. 'What on earth did you do?' Tony asked. 'Well, what would you have done?' he said. 'I put the train into reverse and drove back again!' He didn't get a medal for that, but Tony thinks he should have done!

Harriet was known as 'Ally', a nickname whose origin is lost in the mists of time. It was probably Alfred's affectionate abbreviation of 'Harry', short for Harriet. She was always just a little bit old-fashioned. When her husband came home one day and told her about the invention of a device that carried sound through the air called 'the wireless', she immediately shut all the windows because she didn't want other people to hear what they were saying.

Ally wasn't Jewish by birth, but she took on Jewish ways, so that her answer to every situation was to feed people. Whenever her grandsons went to see her – and she was 93 when she died – the first thing she'd say was, 'What would you like? I've got a nice tin of peaches.' Then she would recite a litany of comestibles, from a cold sausage to pineapple and cream.

Rosa, Cyril and Mark were living with Alfred and Ally in Tollet Street when the twins were born. Rosa – or Rosie, as Geoff insisted on calling her, although she much preferred her proper name – was very hard-working, resourceful and utterly determined to move up the social ladder. The family name was originally Ham, but as Cyril and Rosie started moving up a few rungs they changed it to the more impressive-sounding Hamilton, and the boys, then aged about 11, were made to sit at the table to practise writing their new surname.

'She was a wonderful woman,' says Tony, 'but I have to say she was also the world's greatest snob. She used to buy us clothes which she and Cyril really couldn't afford, and which we didn't need, just because the neighbours' kids weren't dressed quite as well. One day she bought us what we called the Lord Halifax overcoats. Lord Halifax used to wear a long Crombie overcoat right down to the ground, and she bought us two coats like that which must have cost a fortune. We hated them. We were embarrassed by them, and the boys at school made terrible fun of us. So we decided we would lose them. We left them in the park. She did berate us for that, but we just couldn't wear those coats. They were terrible. But at least we had the satisfaction of knowing that there was some down-and-out now going around Hertfordshire with *two* Crombie overcoats. That's more than Lord Halifax had!'

Her concern with appearances didn't stop even when they had grown up. When Geoff had just started work at the age of 22, Rosie said to him one day, 'You can't go into town like that! You look as though you work on the land!' Geoff patiently pointed out, 'Rosie, I *do* work on the land!' Perhaps it was part of Geoff's rebellion to be sartorially casual all his life, and it gave him great satisfaction later in life to be voted the worst-dressed man on television.

The boys were not the only ones to suffer. Cyril was also subjected to rigorous scrutiny. 'One day,' Geoff's youngest son Christopher recalls, 'they were going down to the yacht club where they kept their cabin cruiser and Cyril was wearing an old baggy jumper. "You can't go to the yacht club looking like that!" Rosie said. Most men would have given her an argument, but Cyril knew better, so he just went upstairs and put on his tails and dickie bow and came back down. "You can't go to the yacht club looking like that!" Rosie said, so without a word Cyril went upstairs again, changed back into the old baggy jumper and off they went!'

Stephen, who is Geoff's eldest son, believes Cyril survived and enjoyed life with acts of quiet rebellion. 'They had a lampshade that was a glass bowl hanging from the ceiling on chains, and he used to strike a match then flick it up there into the bowl. Ping! And it drove Rosie mad!'

Keeping up appearances mattered very much to Rosie, as Robert Browning, whose family was friendly with the Hamiltons and who was also a contemporary of Geoff's and Tony's at school, recalls. 'I remember Rosa for one reason. She was the sort of person who was great at compliments, and when I saw her one day she said, "I think your father's marvellous. He always wears the same coloured socks and tie!" So do I now, and if I ever find I've put on different coloured socks and tie I always think of Rosa!'

She was extremely, if not obsessively, houseproud, as Stephen recalls. 'When we were kids we weren't allowed to sit on the settee because we would dent the cushions, and when she had a new carpet she put newspapers down on it for a good year or so.' But Rosie, having earned it the hard way, was conscious of the value of money, and she was a formidable adversary when driving a bargain. Once she persuaded a shop to let her have a vacuum cleaner on a home trial. The next day she went back to the shop and said, 'Yes, that's fine. I'll have it. How much?' When they told her, she said, 'I'm not paying that! It's second-hand!' and got it at a discount.

She was also very ambitious for the boys, or at least for the twins. Mark Hamilton doesn't recall any parental pressure on him at all. He thinks he had claimed the role of black sheep of the family so early that when he announced that he wanted to be a professional musician, and not sit the Cambridge University entrance exams as planned, neither Rosie nor Cyril tried to dissuade him, and he was very grateful to them for that. But Rosie wanted Geoff and Tony to be doctors. That was the pinnacle of ambition as far as she was concerned, and she was not pleased when Geoff wanted to make a career in gardening. Cyril, on other hand, took a more positive view. 'If that's what you really want to do,' he told Geoff, 'then do it – but be the best.'

When Geoff was on television, though, no one was more proud, more vociferous and more voluble about his achievements than Rosie. She used to say to perfect strangers, 'Of course, my son is Geoff Hamilton – you know, the television gardener.' Geoff really hated that. He was terribly embarrassed by it and would go out of his way to diffuse it. If anyone asked where he came from he'd call on his best cockney accent and say, 'Dahn the Mile End Road; Charrington's Brewery; first left, first right; Tollet Street; number firty. Know what I mean?' Rosie would be shocked to the core and say, 'There's no need to tell people that, Geoffrey.'

In fairness to Rosie, she and Cyril (or Cy, as the boys called him) had a real struggle to get where they got, and they did very well by dint of hard work and inventiveness, and she was proud of that. She was also extremely proud of the Hamilton name, which is rather surprising since it wasn't hers by birth and only became hers some time after she and Cyril were married. 'Remember you're a Hamilton!' she used to say to her sons and grandsons. 'You can't do that – you're a Hamilton!' Swearing was absolutely taboo in the house, so Geoff and Tony invented an expletive of their own – Ots! – the rudest word they knew which they could use with impunity in Rosie's presence. And they carried on using it right through their lives.

If Rosie were embarrassed by her East End roots, to the extent of persuading her mother to change her surname from Abrahams to Graham after her father had died, then Geoff was very proud of his, although he was only a toddler when the family left Tollet Street. As he told Radio Leicester listeners in 1995, 'The funny thing is that when I go back to the East End of London and hear that very characteristic accent, I feel at home.'

Lynda, Geoff's widow, feels that Rosie was a powerful influence on Geoff, mainly because he reacted so strongly against what he saw as her airs and graces and her desire for respectability, and he was determined to remain an ordinary bloke no matter how successful he became. His son Stephen thinks they clashed because Geoff was very like her in some ways, a strong character with lots of nervous energy and an impatience to get things done. 'I told him how like her he was once, and he said "I know! How do you think that makes me feel?"'

In the spring of 1938, when the twins were 18 months old, Cyril rented a house for the family at 34 New Road, Broxbourne, Hertfordshire. Later on, he was able to buy it for £400. In those days Broxbourne was very rural, with Mr Frogley's farm at the end of the road, which was later to become one of the country's first garden centres, owned and run by Cor van Hage, where Geoff was to get his very first job in horticulture some years later. At first Rosie was horrified – 'What on earth are we doing living out here in the sticks like this?' – but soon grew to love it.

With three growing children, the family needed more space, but the talk of war was another reason for moving out of London. Mark, then aged six, remembers very clearly the day that war was declared. 'The twins, or the boys as they were always known, were under the kitchen table with their heads in the toy cupboard. I was pottering about. Cyril and Rosie were in the room, plus a couple called Ken and Betty Scorer who were staying with us. I remember the radio was playing very serious martial music, and I was depressed by this music. I've never liked depressing classical music since. Then Neville Chamberlain came on and gravely announced we were at war with Germany, at which Rosie and Betty Scorer fell on to the floor, literally in hysterics. We didn't have a clue what war was, so the boys and I just couldn't contain ourselves with all this weird stuff going on, and burst out laughing. Then the two men grabbed hold of their wives and in true 1930s movie style slapped them round the face to bring them to their senses, which creased the three of us up even more! Next, my father went round all the windows with a roll of wide sticky tape and filled in all the gaps, round the back door and over the keyhole. Then he let down the rolled-up blankets that were already suspended over the inner doors. The tap was full on, and he was filling buckets and throwing water all over these blankets, presumably as a precaution against gas attacks or fire, so the kitchen floor was awash and it was soaking out into the hall carpet and up the stairs. The boys and I just fell about laughing. That is my first clear memory of the twins.'

Although they escaped the worst of the war, Broxbourne was only 17 miles from London, and the twins were very much aware of what was happening. Cyril thought it better to tell the boys what was going on because he felt it would be more frightening for them to be kept in the dark. Occasionally a child in the class would not turn up at school because their house had been hit by a stray bomb the night before, and they could see dogfights over London, and parts of the city on fire. One day they were standing on the air-raid shelters at school and saw a Messerschmitt shot down by a Spitfire and the pilot bale out. They saw him land by the river and start bundling up his parachute with stones to throw it in the water and sink it. So, filled with excitement, they rushed inside and told the teacher, who phoned the police. 'By the time we got back to the air-raid shelter,' Tony recalls, 'the pilot had disposed of the parachute and was just getting ready to disappear when a police car came along the towpath and caught him. The police came to the school afterwards and congratulated everybody on doing a great service to the nation because we'd helped catch Jerry. It was all very exciting and the boys became John Mills for weeks afterwards!'

Their attempts to aid the war effort weren't always as successful, like the time when they were walking home from school, aged about seven, and discovered an unexploded bomb in a hedgerow. Immediately, Geoff took command and ordered Tony to stay and guard it to keep civilians away, while he, taking the cushier option as usual, ran home to get Dad. Dad was eating sausage and mash at the kitchen table and, because sausages were hard to get in wartime, he was very reluctant to leave them. But when Geoff mentioned 'unexploded bomb' he leapt up, got on his bike and, with Geoff running along behind, set off at full speed. There was Tony marching up and down as ordered, keeping civilians away. Much to the twins' surprise Cyril bent down, picked up the bomb and waved it angrily in their faces. It was an old lavatory ball cock! 'Well, it looked like the bombs that Desperate Dan used to have, in the *Dandy*. It just didn't have BOMB written on it!'

They didn't have an air-raid shelter, but when the sirens went off they used to sleep in the cupboard under the stairs, passing the time by eating chocolate powder, dried egg and dried milk from the large tins of emergency rations stored there, and attempting to flick corn plasters, which they'd found in Cyril's coat pocket, into the downstairs lavatory across the hall. 'It was always a mystery why Cy kept a copious supply of corn plasters in his coat pocket, but we never plucked up the courage to ask.'

At about 2 o'clock one morning, when they were all asleep, they were woken by loud knocking on the front door. It was their grandparents, Alf and Ally, covered in soot and dirt, their clothes all torn, asking if they could put them up. They'd been bombed out. The next day grandfather Alf, a very determined character, found a house to rent nearby and bought a new taxi because the old one had been destroyed in the bombing raid. Two days later he was back in business. He couldn't afford to waste petrol driving to and from Broxbourne every day, so he'd leave the taxi in London and cycle backwards and forwards – 34 miles a day!

Cyril had to register for war work, and when asked what skills he had, said: 'I'm a salesman.' There wasn't a lot of call for salesmen in the forces, so he was asked what he did at school. 'Oh, the normal things,' he said; 'reading, writing and arithmetic.' Still no interest from the registrar. 'What did you do with your hands?' he said, beginning to sound exasperated. 'Well, I did a bit of wood-work,' said Cyril. 'Right,' said the registrar, 'skilled carpenter.' And that's what he did throughout the war. The easiest skill he'd ever acquired, but not so easy to apply. His first job was to repair the wing of a Mosquito that had broken off during a dogfight. It took him weeks – but he achieved it in the end and went on to become quite a passable chippie.

He started working at Broxbourne aerodrome, a small grass strip, and later at de Havilland. He earned very little – about £5 a week – so Rosie worked in a local shop all through the war to supplement the family income. Cyril did odd jobs in the evenings as well. He would do anything to ensure that his family was provided for in very difficult circumstances. Once he repaired an antique bedstead for a wealthy old lady who lived locally in a large house. He told her that the only thing to do with this bedstead was take it all apart and put it back together again, but it would take a long time to do and cost quite a lot of money. She told him to go ahead. What he didn't tell her was that all it needed was re-gluing and cramping, and he spent a week up there, banging on the floor occasionally to make her think he was working hard. When Geoff and Tony found out about this, they were horrified. 'We must have been eight or nine and just beginning to develop a social conscience. But when we protested, he said, "Look, if my family's going hungry and there are people out there who have a lot more than they need, then I see no wrong in helping them to redistribute their wealth – as long as I don't break the law." That was his attitude, his political philosophy if you like.'

Despite the dramas and being deprived of bananas, oranges and toys, Tony remembers their childhood in the war as a very happy time because he had his parents to make him feel safe at home and Geoff always at his side to make him feel secure everywhere else. 'Geoff and I loved the radio, and *Monday Night at 8* was a particular favourite. But we were usually sent to bed at 8 o'clock, so what we used to do was creep across the landing from our bedroom into a corner of the bathroom, where the water pipes went down into the room below. A bomb that had fallen nearby had loosened the plaster a bit, so there was a hole there, and since you couldn't get plaster in the war, it stayed like that. We discovered that if you unscrewed the towel rail, which was an aluminium tube, pushed one end into the hole, and held the other to your ear, you could hear *Monday Night at 8* downstairs. So we'd lie on the floor, taking turns to listen and tell each other what we heard.'

Mark was already at primary school, Broxbourne School, when Geoff and Tony started at the age of five. They did well at school, usually top of the class – Geoff top and Tony second – and for fun used to confuse the teachers by pretending to be the other one. Given they had each other, the twins felt no need to make many close boy friends, but they were both very keen on girls from quite early on. When they were about nine, Tony remembers he and Geoff cycling down St Michael's Road in Broxbourne and Geoff putting it to Tony that it would be much more convenient if he were not in love with Pamela Grist but with Janet Cleverley, because she was a friend of *his* girlfriend, Ann Sykes. And even then he had such charisma that Tony immediately and dutifully fell in love with Janet Cleverley – because Geoff told him to. What's more, he stayed with her for ages – until he was at least ten. (A year's a long time when you're nine.) Her father was a pig farmer, and Tony remembers sitting in the back of his very smelly van talking – you only ever talked in those days – when the doors were flung open and there was a big man in overalls, who said, 'If I ever find you in here again with my daughter, I'll break your back! Get out of here.' So he went, and never saw her again.

They also joined the Boy Scouts, the lst Broxbourne, where Geoff eventually became patrol leader of the Badger Patrol and Tony patrol leader of the Owls, each thoroughly enjoying the experience. They both believed in later life that the Boy Scouts shaped their whole philosophy, teaching them self-reliance, respect for other people and, perhaps most prominent in Geoff's make-up, a passionate belief in the need to preserve and nurture the environment. They both eventually became Queen's Scouts, among the first batch of Queen's Scouts in the country at that time – but only because the King had had the good grace to die just before the event.

Michael Howes, an old friend, remembers Geoff as his patrol leader teaching him how to tie knots. 'It was very strange seeing him 30 years later on television teaching people how to garden in exactly the same clear, easy-to-remember way as he had taught me how to tie a reef knot.' Michael also has memories of Geoff and of what were called 'Wide Games', which were the scouting equivalent of military exercises, for which the whole troop would go off into the countryside. Sometimes the games would be a form of group hide-and-seek, or they would involve clues. 'I remember a Wide Game that Geoff organized on Nazeing Common. Unfortunately, for some reason he provided all the clues in French, so very few of us understood them and it wasn't a huge success.'

Both Geoff and Tony enjoyed the outdoor activities particularly, and indeed spent a lot of their spare time together playing in the woods. Most weekends they'd go off to the woods, build shelters, make fires and often spend the night or the weekend there. When they were older they used to do survival weekends, where they took nothing with them – no food, no water, no cooking pots – except some rope or string, an axe and a knife. They survived on things like hedgehogs cooked in the gypsy way – wrapped in clay and baked in the fire, so that the spines come off in the clay when you break it open. 'It's good meat, hedgehog,' says Tony. 'Tastes a bit like turkey.' It gave them the ability to live close to nature and survive, something that stayed with Geoff all his life. He felt the need to be close to nature, and the fact that he was able to make his living out of it gave him enormous satisfaction.

Geoff's interest in gardening, encouraged by Cyril, also started very young. 'When I was five years old,' Geoff said later, 'I was lucky enough to know what I wanted to do and even more lucky to be right about it. It happens to have turned out to be a job that has given me joy for my entire life.' Lynda believes that Cyril was very clever. 'Unlike a lot of parents, he didn't make the boys do the boring jobs like weeding. Instead he gave them their own patch of garden and got them to grow things like radishes and lettuces, which he bought from them, so then they were free to grow whatever they liked.'

Tony remembers spending weeks digging over a large bed in the vegetable garden that was infested with ground elder and sieving the soil to remove every piece of root. There were no chemicals then, and he didn't know about Bob Flowerdew's old carpet trick, so that was the only way. Geoff, meanwhile, was probably in the greenhouse with Cyril. He was very fond of the greenhouse and he used to grow wonderful chrysanthemums with his dad. In fact they got so obsessive about gardening, and so keen to spare their dear old dad any hard labour, that, during the week before they had to go off to do their National Service, they dug the whole garden (and it was a *big* garden), finishing the final bed on their last night, in the dark, by the light of candles.

Encouraged by their grandfather, Tony and Geoff became keen cyclists too. Tony, the prudent one, saved his pocket money for about two years to buy a Phillips Roadster costing £13. He can remember to this day being in their camp at the bottom of the garden when their mother came down to say that his bike was at the station. 'Geoff and I rushed over and there was this brand-new bike all wrapped in cardboard with the pedals turned in. I was over the moon.' Geoff already had a bike, a second-hand one, because he couldn't save like Tony. He was the expansive one, so he used to go out and spend his pocket money every week. In fact, how much money the boys each had was one of the few things they *were* quite competitive about.

They used to buy books, second-hand books from a shop in Hoddesdon called Lovedays, which was a real treasure cave. They'd spend all Saturday in there sometimes, browsing and finally making the decision about which books to buy. Adventure stories were favourite – Fenimore Cooper and Jack London in particular.

Sometimes the urge to spend on anything at all was overpowering, even for Tony, the careful one. 'I can't imagine why, but we used to buy mapping pens from the stationer's with a little bottle of Indian ink and draw pictures. And if we had a penny over, we'd buy a box of matches with it!' One day, when they were about six, the urge to spend was so strong, and with all their pocket money gone, they succumbed to temptation to steal some money of Rosie's that was lying on the table. They went down to the local sweet shop and asked the woman for 2 ounces of this and 2 ounces of that, and put their money on the counter. But what the two naughty little boys didn't realize was that the coins were only tokens from a local grocer's – the 'divi', as it was then called. Oh, the humiliation.

'But to be honest, apart from things like the bike, money didn't feature much in our lives at all then, and that was something that stayed with Geoff. One of the things he often used to say was, "Don't worry about it. It's only money." I'd say to him, "Come on, you've got this lovely house, 10 acres of garden and a big Land Rover Discovery parked over there. Don't tell me it doesn't mean anything to you!" and he would reply, "Well, yes, it does mean a lot to me, but if I suddenly got a million pounds I wouldn't know what to do with it. After all, I've got two spades and who could ask for anything more!"'

Geoff's love of music, another passion that was to stay with him all his life, also began very early. When they were seven he and Tony joined the choir at St Augustine's, the local Church of England church, encouraged, though not dragooned into it, by Rosie and by the fact that they got paid half a crown (12½p) for weddings. As Geoff said in an interview with Radio Leicester in 1995, the choir did two things for him. First, it broadened his interest in music and gave him a love for choral works, and second, it gave him his very first opportunity for performing. 'I was terrified of appearing before groups of people, and I have never lost that. People think that because you're on television you must be pretty good at performing in front of audiences, but I don't think I am. On television, you're performing to three or four people – you forget about the five million watching at home. But with audiences you get an instant reaction, and that's a bit different.'

Neither of them was keen on the ruffs and surplices they had to wear, although they were aware that they appealed to women of all ages, and like all choirboys they did their fair share of messing around during services. They used to make paper aeroplanes and throw them across to each other, and they also had in the choir stalls a little stack of comic books, pinched from Woolworth, that they used to read during the sermon. Their behaviour can't have been that bad, though, because they were each eventually made top boy of their respective sides of the choir, Geoff of decani and Tony of cantoris.

A fellow choirboy, David Hislop, who became a professional musician and presented the BBC2 series on folk guitar playing called *Hold Down a Chord*, remembers the day Geoff was appointed top boy of decani. 'There was a tradition that the new top boy always got christened in the river. Geoff said to us, "Look, give me a 100 yards' start, that's only fair." So we did, and he led us a merry dance, but eventually we caught up with him!' David Hislop has other musical memories of Geoff as a boy and, indeed, has reason to be grateful to him. 'I remember being at a party at one of the Hamiltons' neighbours. Geoff and Tony were singing together in harmony songs like 'Way Down Upon the Swanee River', 'Camptown Ladies' and 'Clementine' and Geoff was playing a ukulele. It just rooted me to the spot. Then I remembered that we had an old ukulele at home under the stairs, so I got it repaired and that started my guitar career. Later on, I wanted a guitar. Geoff had a four-stringed one like a uke only bigger, and my parents bought it from Geoff for my Christmas present one year.'

The Scouts provided Geoff with an opportunity to perform in the Gang Shows that the troop put on in the mid-1950s. Michael Howes remembers Geoff with the skiffle group he had formed playing the ukulele and singing the old Lonnie Donegan hit 'Freight Train'.

Geoff's interest in the guitar carried on intermittently until his early twenties. Mark recalls owning a jazz guitar that Geoff wanted and eventually persuaded him to swap for his own steel-string acoustic guitar, which Mark still has. In February 1957 he wrote to Mark from RAF Wildenrath in Germany, where he was doing his national service, 'I'm going to take up the guitar seriously, and I wonder if you could send me out a little elementary tuition. You know, music and scales and things. I tried to pick it up from that Ivor Mairantz tutor, but it jumps from how to hold the darned thing to augmented thirteenths and diminished sevenths etc. and I just couldn't get a grip of it. If you could find the time to write out the fingering and the main scales I'd need, I would be eternally grateful. My musical faith is rapidly being shattered by the Haleys and Hughes etc. so for God's sake hurry up. Thanks a lot.' Unlike many young people of his day, Geoff was clearly not impressed by the new rock 'n' roll at all. 'How's the old act going?' he wrote in the same letter. 'Can't really say I envy you 'cos Rock and Roll ain't the best thing for a musician's nerves and it looks like the next craze is going to be only a little better.'

Mark, by this time a professional musician playing bass in bands like Mick Mulligan's Magnolia Jazz Band and backing visiting jazz singers like Frances Day, was another huge musical influence in Geoff's life. Mark had fallen in love with jazz at the age of ten when he heard the Artie Shaw orchestra on the radio, and as Geoff grew up the house was filled with the music of the jazz greats – Gerry Mulligan, Ella Fitzgerald, Chet Baker, Stephane Grappelli, Cleo Laine (for whom Mark did the photography for her first record sleeve) and a host of others. Later on, when Mark was playing at Ronnie Scott's club in London's Soho, Geoff used to go to see him there and got to meet some of these legends.

Classical music was a part of Geoff's childhood too. Rosie introduced the twins to it at home, and when they both passed the eleven-plus and went to Hertford Grammar School they had to listen to a classical record for 20 minutes after assembly each day. 'For the first year or so I hated it,' Geoff said. 'I'd sit there and fidget and think, "Who wants to listen to this old-fashioned stuff?" But gradually, gradually it seeped into my brain until eventually I began to look forward to it, and ever since I've loved it. I've been so grateful for that because it's such an important part of my life.'

Later in life, when Geoff fell on hard times and basically was starting again from scratch, according to Lynda his essential items were a kettle, some tins of beans, his record player and his Beethoven and Vivaldi records.

Geoff was full of praise for Hertford Grammar School in other ways. 'It was a great school in the old tradition and I greatly mourn the passing of those schools. It was a fairly free-and-easy place, but they really pushed the knowledge into you in an extremely interesting way. I can remember, for example, when I was interested in horticulture I was studying zoology and botany. As part of the exam, we had to do a project on ecology and I decided I wanted to do something about the river. My biology master said, "Great! Nobody's done that before. Let's go and look at it now." This was lunchtime, so we jumped on the back of his motorbike and off we went to look at it. It was that sort of thing that really encouraged you.'

Both the boys were also deeply influenced by their headmaster, Tom Bunt. He was a man who had only one great weakness – he just loved his boys and his job. Even when he was about to discipline one of the boys he would stretch out his long, thin arms, his gown flapping around him, and start by straightening the boy's tie. Just an affectionate gesture that defused a potentially frightening situation.

Many good teachers were there, most of them with extraordinarily individual characteristics. 'Biff' Clouting, the physics master, for instance, would pride himself on the fact that when he caned a boy he could get every stroke in *exactly* the same place. As recipients, the twins could vouch for that. 'Masher' Martin, geography, had an old banger of a car that was falling to pieces; it was Geoff who painted on the back 'THIS IS THE BACK'. Jimmy Irwin, English, was a born Shakespearean who would growl at misbehaving boys, 'Thou monkey. Thou varlet,' and would stride up and down between the rows of desks, beating the slackers with his only arm and pronouncing, 'You're wasting your time and your parents' money.' In an environment like that, how could any boy not develop his character and his joy of life?

John Morphew, who was in the twins' year at school, remembers them as being very small and skinny and fighting a lot. 'They always seemed to be scrapping over by the rifle range, but if you were daft enough to intervene they'd both turn on you!' Again, because they had each other they didn't need to make lots of friends, but they had a few. Robert Browning was one of them. 'When we were all about 15 or 16, a mutual friend, Clive Darlow, and I got to know Geoff and Tony because we formed a sort of boys' club, called the Rapide Club after the de Havilland aeroplane. Clive's dad was the secretary of Broxbourne Flying Club where they had a Rapide. They used to send it up for the Observer Corps to spot and if there were empty seats we used to go up for a trip. But mainly we met in a caravan and solved the problems of the day.'

Tony doesn't recall any flying and he remembers its aims as somewhat less lofty. 'They were primarily to assess and appraise the talent of the village. Initially we met in our house, but soon after we bought a trailer and built a plywood caravan on top of it, where we met once a week. We drew up a chart with the names of all the girls we knew down one side and scores along the top from one to ten and we'd give each girl a mark out of ten. This was reassessed once a week – we felt it was important to keep on top of things! It was an unwritten rule that if one of the girls on the list was a member's current girl friend he gave her ten and the others gave her nothing. When she fell out of favour, she went into the pot and took her chances with the rest! We went to dances together as well. One would climb in through the gents' toilet window and let the others in through the back door. It was considered gross negligence if you didn't end up taking a girl home and at the next meeting we would then swap stories – with a large degree of boasting and exaggeration, of course. We also used to dabble in the occult, but the difficulty was that we all found it so funny we could never accomplish any of it. We'd try table-tapping. We'd sit in the dark around this little card table with our fingers touching, but then you'd feel someone's knees trembling with suppressed laughter and we'd all break up. I'm afraid we never succeeded in getting through to The Other Side.'

Like many schools immediately after the war, Hertford Grammar still had the allotments that had been created in the school grounds

Geoff, Mark and Tony. Or is it Tony, Mark and Geoff? Even Tony isn't sure.

By the age of five, when the twins started school, Geoff (left) has a slightly broader face than Tony.

Four generations with Geoff (front right): Great Grandmother seated behind him, Grandma Ally (far right), Rosie in the centre, Mark and Tony (front left).

The family on the beach: Geoff in the centre, Mark on the left and Tony on the right.

Keep the campfires burning: Geoff is in the centre, saucepan in hand.

All teeth and eyes: Geoff is on the left, but you can see why the teachers at Hertford Grammar found it so hard to tell them apart.

We're all going on a summer holiday…in school uniforms and homburg hat.
Geoff is next to his father Cyril.

Geoff waits his turn to receive his First Class badge from the District Commissioner.

Geoff persuaded to pose in Dylan Thomas mode by Mark early in Mark's photographic career.

Coxed fours on the River Lea; Geoff as cox telling the others what to do.

Geoff (left) and Tony find something to laugh about during national service.

The diploma in horticulture course at Writtle College 1958–9. Geoff is in the second row, third from the left.

to help feed the boys and their families when food was scarce, and any boys who were interested could take one on. Geoff and Tony had an allotment along with another boy in the class, Martin Philips. 'They were both very good gardeners,' he recalls, 'but I wasn't. I'd sow a row of peas or whatever and stick in a few elder twigs to mark the row, but the only thing that grew for me were the elder twigs!' 'Martin', said Tony, 'had the finest crop of elder trees in Hertfordshire. He should have joined the Forestry Commission.'

They both took part in the debating society, but Geoff's silly sense of humour somewhat debased its lofty aims. It was he, for example, who established a 'tradition' that Candlemas should be celebrated by debating among a mass of candles. So all the boys dutifully arrived with three or four candles each and the debate ended with the library floor a mass of candle wax. It was a tradition that died an early death. They also appeared in the occasional school play, often produced or led by John Tydeman, who later became Head of Drama at the BBC. Tony remembers a production of *Richard III* in which he and Geoff played minor parts. They were, he recalls, pretty rotten actors, and, as they both had very skinny legs, appearing in tights was always a source of some grief. In fact, many years later, when Geoff was invited to appear as a seventeenth-century gardener at the Lord Mayor's Show which involved wearing tights, he managed to hide his embarrassment, and his legs, with a pair of thigh boots.

Having always been top of the class at primary school, it had come as a bit of a shock, according to Tony, to find themselves with other boys more intelligent than they were. They couldn't really cope with that, so they resorted to having fun rather than learning. They didn't do brilliantly, but they did all right. In fact, for a time, Tony did better than Geoff and was in a higher stream, but they took advantage of being in different forms temporarily to swap places just to see if any of the masters noticed. They never did.

When they were about 14 Geoff became very ill. He had been taken to hospital with appendicitis and had been given either the wrong drugs or too much of the right drugs, so that he was unconscious, and there was a real danger that he was going to die. 'I came down one morning,' Tony says, 'and I just had a feeling that he was through it, that he was going to be all right. There was no blinding flash of light or anything – just a feeling – so I told Rosie to ring the hospital. She did, and they said Geoff had just come round. I must say that was the only time in my life that I've ever felt anything like a telepathic experience – a concept neither of us really believed in.'

Rosie and Cyril were very keen ballroom dancers, winning medals and in Rosie's case being qualified to teach, so that Geoff and Tony were both taught to dance and made to attend many Masonic Ladies' night dinner-dances in their youth. They hated the lessons at the dancing-school, partly because they were uncomfortable with the pretensions and partly because everybody called them 'our twins' – an expression that seemed to rob them of all their individuality. So they decided to find a way out of it. Every Christmas the dancing-school would have a party and everybody was asked to put a present on the Christmas tree. They were normally knitted toilet-roll holders or fluffy toys, but the boys took a trip to Leather Lane market in London and bought some wide 'kipper' ties with naked women painted on them. The reaction was such that they were never asked to return and were able to join the rowing club on the River Lea at Broxbourne instead.

Here their small stature and skinny build made them ideal coxes, and they steered boats and, from the age of 13 to 16, derived great pleasure from shouting at grown men. 'We had great times, because we were mixing with people older than ourselves. They looked after us really well – they'd take us to regattas and pay for us to stay in nice hotels. They also did two other things for us – enlarged our vocabulary and introduced us to the demon drink!' They trained hard, rowing most nights all year round, even rowing in the dark in winter with the aid of a bicycle lamp strapped to the front of the boat. It could be very dicey, as it was on the night when the four that Tony was coxing was going flat out and didn't see a pleasure boat ahead. 'We ran over its it bows, but while there was no damage done we gave the man in the boat a real fright. He seemed to think it was my fault and said, "When you get back to the clubhouse, I'll be waiting and I'll have you!" which put the fear of God into me. And sure enough, when we got back to the club, there he was waiting for me on the hard. I got out of the boat followed by four extremely burly oarsmen who said, "So what are you going to do about it?" and the man just slunk away.'

By the time they were 15 they started to row in earnest, usually in the same boat, Tony at stroke and Geoff at bow. In later years, when they were working hard physically each day, they became supremely fit – but, Tony says, they were still lousy oarsmen. 'We didn't do too badly, though. One year we rowed in the Head of the River Race, which was held on the same day as the Boat Race in those days. We started 265th and we finished 127th, which meant we'd rowed past quite a lot of other boats.'

The rowing club also became a major focus for their social life, and it was there when he was about 17 that Geoff met the first love of his life, Marilyn Early (now Norvell). She remembers with great affection the dances at the rowing club, where they played games such as Pass the Thimble; the thimble was balanced on a straw and so the game involved lots of close clutching – purely for balance, of course! 'He was great fun and everyone loved him, but he had a way of making you feel that you had a special place in his life. He was romantic too. He bought me my first watch – gold-plated and very stylish – and then, sadly, I hopped into the bath with it on so that was the end of that. I remember his skinny legs and his passion for growing chrysanthemums at the bottom of their garden. In fact, it was Geoff who got me interested in gardening, and he's the reason I'm working in a garden centre now.'

Cricket was another favourite sport, probably because Cyril had played for the local club – 'I've watched him get out first ball more times than I care to remember!' said Tony – and the boys used to go along to act as scorers. They remained keen spectators into adult life. Tony still goes to test matches when he can, and in spare moments on location filming days Geoff could often be found in his car listening to *Test Match Special* on the radio. 'One of the very few things about Geoff that used to drive me mad when we were younger,' Tony recalls, 'was that whenever he said something was great, he'd always mime playing a cricket stroke and make the sound of leather on willow with his tongue!'

Perhaps their finest cricketing hour came during one of the annual staff-*v.*-boys cricket matches on Parents' Day at Hertford Grammar. Geoff borrowed a French horn from the music room and Tony borrowed a trumpet, and they hid on either side of the field, each in one of the large shrubberies. Just as one of the masters was about to bowl, Geoff would give a loud blast on the French horn, and all the prefects and some of the masters went running towards the shrubbery where the sound came from. But just before they got there, Tony would give a blast on the trumpet and they'd all turn round and go running the other way. The parents were not too impressed, but Geoff and Tony thought it was great fun. They did get found out and sent to the headmaster who, having stretched out his arms and straightened their ties, found it rather amusing too, so they only got reprimanded.

The biology labs were also a source of potential mischief-making. Once, Geoff filled the glass bowl lampshades with water and tadpoles so that when the lights were switched on, weird shadows wriggled their way across the walls. Above the biology labs, which were in a separate building from the rest of the school, was a room that the sixth-formers were allowed to use as a common room for private study between lessons. One day, in boredom, Geoff took up one of the floorboards and discovered underneath a light fitting with a flex hanging through the ceiling into the room below. It was quite a big hole and through it he could see a lesson going on in the room downstairs. So Geoff began to pull the light, which was hanging above the master's head very slowly up and down. The boys very quickly saw what was happening and began to follow the light with their eyes, and eventually, of course, the master twigged what was going on. Geoff and his friends heard footsteps tearing up the stairs, so Geoff slammed the floorboard back into place, sat down and started writing away furiously. The master burst in and said, 'OK, Hamilton, so how do you control the light downstairs?' 'Well, sir,' Geoff said, 'there's a switch by the door. You just switch it up and down!' They got a detention for that but felt it was well worth it.

Perhaps not surprisingly, neither Geoff nor Tony was made a prefect. When they left school the headmaster called them into his study to explain why. He said it had been good having them in the school and 'You just seemed to be having too much fun, and who was I to spoil it?' They thought that was fair enough. 'We did have too much fun,' says Tony, 'and I think we probably wasted our time at school and could have done better. You needed three A-levels to go to university, and we only got two, but since we both wanted to go to college – Geoff to do horticulture, me to do agriculture – that was OK by us.'

Despite Rosie's disapproval, Geoff had made the decision that he would make a career in horticulture, and, indeed, had already started work on Saturdays and in the school holidays at the small nursery that had just started up on the corner of New Road. Its owner was Dutchman Cornelius (Cor) van Hage, who with his two sons William and John now runs the hugely successful van Hage Garden Company just outside Ware in Hertfordshire.

'He was an extremely nice lad,' Cor recalls, 'and we got on like a house on fire from the very start because we shared a similar sense of humour. I'd pull his leg and he'd give as good as he got, and the relationship stayed the same right up until the time that he died. He was a cheeky little beggar in the nicest sense and always had a funny answer ready.

'Geoff had to do everything because we were such a small business, but he was particularly good with customers, very good at talking to people – in fact, a very good salesman, like his father. In selling, I believe personality is almost as important as knowledge, if not more so. If people like you, they can forgive your ignorance if you don't know something. But Geoff also picked things up very quickly. Once he had learnt about a plant, he knew it. So if he learnt about rhododendrons for a couple of weeks he would sell nothing else, till I had to say to him, "Geoff, there are also other plants!"'

By the time Geoff had taken his A-levels in botany and zoology in the summer of 1954, he had a place at Writtle College in Chelmsford to study horticulture, while Tony had a place to study agriculture. 'It didn't occur to us to apply to different places. I did get a prospectus from the Royal Agricultural College at Cirencester, but that seemed too upper crust for words. Writtle was the one that appealed, partly because we could get home very easily and partly because my girlfriend Christina (who became my first wife) was teaching in Chelmsford too.'

Before they could start their college courses, though, there was not only a year's work experience to be done but also a compulsory two years at that branch of the university of life known as national service.

CHAPTER TWO

YOUNG MAN

During his year's pre-college work experience, Geoff worked in a tomato nursery, where he learnt a great deal about disbudding tomatoes but not a lot else, and for Thomas Rochford, who used to be one of the country's largest houseplant specialists. Tony worked at the latter, too, in the holidays and remembers it as a truly awful job. He was put in a greenhouse 200 feet (61 m) long and on either side, stretching as far as the eye could see, would be, say, aphilandras. 'They'd say, "Right, pot these on," and you'd say, "What, all of them?" and they'd say, "All of them."' In Tony's case, it would take the whole time he was there.

Geoff went back to work for Cor van Hage, who was developing his nursery on the corner of New Road in Broxbourne and, most unusually at that time, had created a show garden with thousands of bulbs and a windmill made in Holland. He had one other member of staff then, a fellow Dutchman called Jim, but he needed more help, and someone like Geoff who already knew the business was ideal. 'Because money was very tight, we took on any other work we could get, like a few landscaping jobs in the area, and Geoff helped me with that. We did some Roman Catholic churches, thanks to the local parish priest who was in charge of the money to give to various churches to spend on lawns, trees and plants. Then we did a housing estate in Royston – our first big job. We got £2500 to £3000 for it, which was a lot of money in those days.

'I remember one job we did together, Geoff and I. We wanted a particular conifer for a garden – an *Abies koreana*, with superb purple cones – and we couldn't find one in a nursery anywhere. But we had seen one in a garden in Broxbourne that we used to drive past all the time. So one day we decided that we would go and ask the owner if we could buy it from him. I couldn't ask, because I'd have felt very awkward, so I persuaded Geoff to do it. I said, "Tell him that you must have it because you've fallen in love with it." Geoff said, "Shall I say it's for my mother's birthday?" and I said "No, say it's for her funeral – that'll have more impact!" Anyway, I parked a few yards down the road and watched from a safe distance. Geoff knocked on the door, and it was opened by this very large man in a vest. I saw Geoff smiling, being charming and gesticulating towards this little conifer as he talked and then I saw the man step forward rather aggressively with his hand raised, and a startled Geoff step back rather quickly. The man took another step forward and Geoff took two more steps backwards, then turned and fled. Apparently, the man was not at all amused by our offer and told Geoff to get out of it, or words to that effect. He was a conifer specialist himself, and it had taken him 20 years to get the tree to that stage! When Geoff came to give a talk at our present garden centre in Ware a few years ago, he told that story, so the experience had obviously left a deep impression.'

Jim, Cor's assistant, was also a great influence on Geoff, both horticulturally and socially. They didn't paint the town red, because neither of them had any money, but they laughed a lot and had endless ribald conversations about the customers. Geoff's lasting memory of Jim is that he was so poor that he had to take some lemonade bottles back to recover the deposit before he could pay for his marriage licence.

At the end of his year's work experience, Geoff had to join up for two years' national service. Mark had already done his national service in the RAF, where he had not only been trained as a photographer but had also learnt to play the double bass. He recommended to Geoff and Tony that they follow in his footsteps, on the grounds that there is very little 'bull' in the RAF, and if you had to spend two years doing something you didn't particularly want to do then you might as well make life as easy for yourself as you could.

'Most people went into the army,' Tony recalls, 'and so it was slightly more difficult to get into the RAF, but Mark advised us what to say. When the recruiting chap asked us why we wanted to join the air force we should say, "Firstly, because my father and brother were both in the air force, sir, so there's a family history in the service, and secondly because we believe it to be the finest fighting force in the world." We did as he suggested, and amazingly they swallowed it.'

Geoff thought that after 19 years spent virtually joined at the hip and, for at least some of them, dressed identically, it might be nice to be separated for a change. 'But in the forces,' he told the *Daily Mail* in 1995, 'they clipped your papers together if you were identical twins because they thought you'd die if the other one wasn't there. And of course they dressed us the same, so we were straight back to square one!' They looked so alike in uniform that once, when Geoff was handed both his own and Tony's photo-identity cards, he had to check the signatures to know which one to hand over and which one to keep.

Unlike Mark, who had gone into the RAF so determined to be a photographer that for his six choices of trade he put down 'photographer' each time, neither Geoff nor Tony had any clear idea of what they wanted to do. 'I thought I'd do something clerical or administrative,' said Tony, 'but they told us we could either be cooks or wireless mechanics, so we said, "Wireless mechanics, please."'

First, though, they were sent off to RAF Hednesford near Cannock Chase for eight weeks' square-bashing. 'That was fun too,' Tony recalls, 'because we just couldn't take it seriously – all that throwing rifles about and stamping your feet. It seemed such a silly thing to do.' As a result he became known as Laughing Boy. 'On one occasion, when I really couldn't take it seriously, I remember the corporal thrusting his face right into mine – they do that, you know; it's just like it is in all those Leslie Thomas books – and said, "You're bloody Laughing Boy, aren't you?" "No, corporal," says I, because I knew Geoff would back me up. He said, "Yes, you are! You're bloody Laughing Boy." I said again, "No, corporal, I'm not." Then he really blew his top – they're very neurotic, these people, obsessed with their power – and he was ranting on until Geoff stepped smartly forward and said, "I'm Laughing Boy, corporal." He looked at the two of us, from one to the other and back again, and he just didn't know what to do. Confusion reigned, with people falling about with laughter, and the poor old corporal knew he'd met his match. I think maybe we got a couple of days' washing up in the cookhouse for it, but basically we got away with it!'

At the passing-out parade at the end of eight weeks' training, the station commander saw them both together for the first time, then came across and said, 'Now I've solved my problem.' He had been driving into camp one day and saw one of them walking in through the gate, then he drove right through the camp (and it was a very big camp) up to one of the billets and there was what appeared to be the same airman walking into the billet ahead of him. 'Before today,' he told them, 'I could not understand how you'd managed to do it! Now I know.'

After the square-bashing came eight weeks' training in their chosen trade – wireless mechanics. 'We did learn a bit about wireless,' Tony says, 'but I've forgotten all of it now. In fact, we forgot what we'd learnt pretty quickly, so when we got to work with real aircraft we would apply what we called 'the drop test'. If you had a set that wasn't working properly, you would simply drop it on the floor, and if it then worked you put it back again. If it didn't, you sent it back for a major service. So we really didn't do very much in the way of actual repairs.'

With hindsight, Geoff enjoyed national service immensely. 'You go in dreading it, and the first few weeks are pretty grim because you are feeling pretty homesick and you're with all these strange people, and people are shouting at you all the time. Eventually, of course, you learn to cope with all this stuff, and the great thing about it is that you meet people from all walks of life and you're thrown together like it or not, living in the same billet, going out together, working together, and it's jolly good for you because it really does broaden the mind. I had some great times, or what I can remember of them because I wasn't sober all the time.'

And, of course, they had each other, something for which Tony remembers being particularly grateful when they were both posted to RAF Wildenrath in Germany, close to the Dutch border, once their basic training was over. 'It was the first time we'd ever been abroad – kids didn't go abroad then like they do now – and I remember finding ourselves outside this hangar on Christmas Eve. It was snowing, and there was a railway line, curving away into pine trees. It looked just like a scene from a war film, so that you almost expected to see cattletrucks loaded with prisoners come round the bend. It was very depressing, but of course having Geoff there made it all right because we buoyed each other's spirits up.'

They stayed close, even sleeping in adjoining beds in the billet. People were amused by the fact that they used to talk to each other in their sleep, and answer each other too, and never know anything about it. They were also able to back each other up when necessary. Tony recalls a time when Geoff had gone out to service a radio and had left his tool bag behind in a dangerous position which could have compromised the safety of the plane. 'It could have caused a crash, so what he'd done was a very serious offence – he could have been sentenced to time in the glasshouse for it – but fortunately the person who went out to service the radio when the plane came back was me, so I just took it back to him and told him to look after himself!'

Tony wasn't around the day that the first prototype Vulcan bomber landed, and was escorted by RAF police Land Rovers to a special bay. Geoff had to go to find the radio on it and make sure it was working properly. 'But he didn't even know how to switch the thing on – it was considered too secret for the provision of a manual. So there he was confronted by a huge console of controls, and he just started pushing buttons at random. Unfortunately, one of them was the undercarriage warning signal, so the air was suddenly rent by a deafening hooter, and he found himself surrounded by police Land Rovers filled with large, stern, armed policemen. Very shamefacedly he had to return to his section with the radio unchecked.'

Although they had used the fact that they were identical twins to great advantage in the past, the RAF gave them undreamt-of opportunities – because in uniform it was totally impossible to tell them apart. 'We used to work on the same squadron, though on opposite 12-hour shifts, but since the air force had hardly any aeroplanes, we never worked for more than about four hours per shift. So we would arrange for one of us to fly home for a spot of unofficial leave – you could hitch rides back to the UK easily enough. We'd both go out to service the aircraft with our tool bags, then Geoff would slip off his overalls. I'd stuff them into my tool bag, we'd service the radio, then I'd walk back to the squadron while Geoff stayed on the plane to fly home. I'd then work both shifts until he came back. Then I'd walk out to the plane with my tool bag and Geoff's overalls, he'd slip them on, and we'd both walk back to the squadron together. That was the only potentially risky time, because there were two of us where there should only have been one, but nobody ever noticed. Geoff and I frequently stayed away for two weeks at a time.'

The other really tricky time was pay parade, when both Hamiltons would be called out to collect their pay one after the other, since the list was strictly alphabetical. 'What I used to do was go up to collect my money, coming smartly to attention in front of the officer in charge, saluting and shouting, "2758984 LAC Hamilton, sir!" and then walk back. But the problem was that Geoff's name came immediately after mine, so we had to arrange for someone in the front rank to have a fit or a coughing attack or some other disaster, just to cause a diversion. This gave me time to rush round the back, then step forward again, come smartly to attention, salute and shout, "2758996 LAC Hamilton, sir!" – and collect his money as well. Although everyone remembers their service number, I don't suppose many people know their brother's as well as their own.'

It wasn't only the RAF that the twins managed to fool. Sometimes, just for fun, they'd play games at local dances. One of them would ask a girl to dance and then spin her some fantastic tale. For example, Geoff once told a girl he was the son of Lord Hamilton of Dalkeith, who owned 30,000 acres in Scotland and had a large herd of Aberdeen Angus cattle. Then he would take the girl back to her seat, and a few minutes later it would be Tony's turn to go to ask for a dance. Of course, she would think she was dancing with the same chap, and Tony's task was then to pick up the story from where Geoff had left off, without having any idea about what he had already told her. It was a great test of inventiveness, and they got their faces slapped more than once. 'I suppose it was rather cruel, but then it's the kind of thing you do when you're young. I think our manners improved in later life.'

On one occasion, though, the consequences could have been more embarrassing. While they were in the RAF, before being posted to Germany, Tony had met a girl at a dance and fallen madly in love. He had asked her for a date and was planning to hitchhike home to meet her. They earned only 16 shillings (80p) a week, and the bus fare home was exactly 16 shillings, leaving no money to spend on the date. That night there were hundreds of other airmen trying to hitch-hike from the camp, and it was taking ages to get a lift. He became very anxious that he wouldn't make it, and he knew that if he stood her up on their first date, that would be that. So he rang his stalwart *doppelgänger* Geoff, who was at home, and asked if he would go in his place. He agreed, and he went and all was well. 'The only thing I didn't like about it,' said Tony, 'is that until the day he died he never told me what happened. Obviously, on subsequent dates I couldn't ask her anything about it, so to this day I still don't know!'

During the mid-1950s, when Geoff and Tony were doing their national service, some RAF stations in Germany had their own pig farms because it was the simplest way to provide pork for the servicemen. Since British bases were considered British territory, buying meat from German farms would have meant going through all sorts of import regulations. Tony had already decided he wanted to be a farmer and had some knowledge of pigs, so he applied to run the pig farm at RAF Wildenrath and got the job. 'It was great because you got so many perks. I managed to convince the officer in charge, who knew nothing about pigs, that the only cure for sick pigs was brandy, so I used to get a chit for a bottle of brandy from the stores every week. Geoff and some of the other boys used to come to the farm to play cards, eat pigs' trotters and drink brandy. It was the greasiest deck of cards you've ever seen!

'In fact, I got away with murder, and nobody said anything to me because they knew that if they did they were unlikely to get their pork ration. So the phrase grew up, as a joke really, "You can't touch me. I work on the station farm!" One day I was in the headquarters drawing out money or something. I was smoking, and my hair was nearly down to my shoulders when the station warrant officer saw me and bawled at me, "Hamilton, get your bloody hair cut," and without thinking I said, "You can't touch me. I work on the station farm!" Much to my surprise he said, "Oh, so you do. Sorry!"

'I also used to draw tea and coffee from the stores, and, since it was hard to come by just across the border in Holland, I got the four Dutch workers on the farm to smuggle it across for me in exchange for a 10 per cent cut. I was King Rat in those days. I'd never do it now. I have a real dread of breaking the law.'

One day Tony had a 'Dear John' from his girlfriend. Lots of servicemen got them, being so far from home, but he was really cut up about it because he was deeply in love with this girl. He told Geoff all about it and Geoff said, 'Tell you what you want to do. You don't want to mope about it. What you need now is a good fight!' They didn't hit each other, but just wrestled each other in the snow. Afterwards, Tony felt a great deal better. It was just the therapy he needed. Then Geoff said, 'What you want to do now is hitch a flight home. I'll run the farm and cover for you. Go and see her and pin her ears back!' So he did just that – went home, pinned back her ears and it was all on again. That was typical of the support they gave each other.

In 1956 Geoff but not Tony was posted to Suez, a cause of no little anxiety to the latter. Geoff came back to the UK, got kitted out and was then sent on two weeks' embarkation leave. By the end of his leave the crisis was over, so he'd just had two weeks' holiday and then returned to Germany without witnessing a shot fired in anger.

At times, Geoff found service life tedious in the extreme. 'Life here is really grim,' he wrote to his brother Mark in February 1957. 'I'm bored to tears all the time. Fortunately, Rosenmontag, which is the big German carnival season, is nearly upon us and just in time. Monday next is the big night and believe me the Chelsea Arts Ball just isn't in it. They go absolutely mad, and it's a week of absolute debauch. The main idea is that the women hold complete sway and can do what they like – and of course no one complains except the odd husband here and there. I reckon on going on leave on 8 April, and I couldn't have timed it worse (or should it be "worser"?). I shall just miss Gerry Mulligan and I'd have given my right arm to see him. Anyway, he's doing a tour of Germany afterwards so I might get in on that.'

But it was by no means all bleak, and Geoff's sons remember with great amusement the stories he used to tell about national service days. 'He was always telling us about a chap called Pateman,' Nick, Geoff's middle son, recalls. 'He was one of life's losers, the only man on the squadron who couldn't get his beret to lie flat at the side – it always stuck out at an angle of 90 degrees to his head. They all had to do bayonet training, which consisted of tearing down a hill, screaming at the top of their military voices and sticking the bayonet into a sack of straw suspended on a wooden frame. Well, this in itself was funny enough, but imagine the joy when Pateman tripped down the hill, making a noise like a pregnant hamster, and tentatively prodded the sack with his bayonet, eventually penetrating it by 2 inches. Well, the corporal in charge just blew a fuse and screamed at poor old Pateman to go back up the hill and do it properly. Next time, Pateman came down the hill as though pursued by the devil himself and screaming like a banshee. Nobody had ever heard anything like it. When he got to the sack he plunged his bayonet in with such ferocity that the whole thing, rifle and all, went right through the sack and the platoon spent ten minutes looking for it on the other side. Pateman was never invited to bayonet practice again.'

But perhaps the boys' favourite Pateman story of all, which they frequently begged Geoff to tell them, involved the flight sergeant drumming it into them all that their rifle was their best friend, to be cherished and cared for, and always at their side. One day he ordered the squadron to be on parade in five minutes with their best friend, and Pateman came staggering out of the billet with his bed on his back. That particular Pateman story was a complete fabrication of Geoff's, Tony says. 'He had a real gift for embellishing, embroidering or just plain making things up. It used to amuse me that I'd tell him about something that had happened to me, and then a few weeks later he'd tell me the exact same story but as if it had happened to him!'

Before they were officially demobbed, they were sent to Chorley in Lancashire for two weeks for a civil defence firefighting course, which was meant to make them fit for the reserve forces in case of war. 'It was great fun, squirting hoses and running up ladders and all this sort of thing, except for the 60-foot escape ladder which went straight up and didn't lean against anything. You had to climb to the top of it and then clip yourself on. You've got a hose over your shoulder, and when you shout, "Water on!" they turn it on, and the hose – and the ladder – rears back alarmingly, and that is scary! That apart, though, it was one of the best and funniest fortnights I've ever spent in my life.

'The other plus was that there were few young men in Chorley – I believe there had been a tragedy involving the local regiment in the Korean War – but there were lots of young women (and Lanca-shire girls were noted for their great beauty), and they used to hold a dance every night of the week and two on Sundays. Some unscrupu-lous young men (though never Geoff or me, of course) would pick up one girl, take her outside and do what men do and then go back for another one. We thought we'd gone to heaven.'

Two years to the day after they enlisted, they were demobbed at RAF Innesworth in Gloucestershire, with all the same people who had joined up with them. 'It was fascinating to see how they had changed. There was one bloke, a farmworker who'd lived in a little cottage outside Dundee, and he had never been further than Dundee in his life before. When he came down to enlist, it was the first time he'd ever been on a train. Because he could drive a tractor, he got a job in the civil engineering unit, driving earth-movers and such like, building airfields all over the world. When he came back, he was just so much more confident, cocky even, and he knew what he wanted out of life. He certainly wasn't going to stay in Dundee!'

In September 1957 they took up the places they had at Writtle College and lived in the same hall of residence, but as they were taking different courses they didn't see much of each other in the day. The chap who sat next to Geoff in lectures was Charles Reed, who now goes by his middle name Richard, and runs a large garden centre and nursery near Chichester. 'He didn't seem particularly good on plant names and identification then, though that was something that clearly changed later in his life, and I remember he was always a bit late with his course work, and would come rushing in at the last minute to try and get things finished. But as for anything going on at the college – Christmas reviews, college concerts, pranks of various kinds – then Geoff was one of the prime movers.' Tony remembers Charles Reed as a chap who endeared himself to everybody – largely through his curiously vague speech, particularly his mixed metaphors, his most memorable being 'dry as a dog' and 'dark as a bone'.

Fellow student Jeremy Savage remembers producing the farce *See How They Run* in which Tony featured as the Reverend Arthur Humphrey and Geoff worked backstage. He also produced a review that Geoff and Tony wrote between them. Geoff sang songs, both alone and with the skiffle group he'd formed at college, the Pussy-footers, and took part in some sketches, while Tony compered the whole thing. 'We were influenced by the Goons a bit, and I had seen a review in London called *Share My Lettuce*, which featured a young man called Kenneth Williams who I felt would go far, and we lifted quite a few ideas from that. I told jokes like, "I was standing outside the Park Lane Hotel the other day – that's where I live, outside the Park Lane Hotel – when this old tramp came up to me and said, 'Spare us some change, guv'nor, I haven't had a bite all day,' so I bit him." It all went down very well.'

Apart from lectures and shows, most of their time at college was spent in the pub, chasing women and generally having a good time. Officially, they had to be back in college by 10 o'clock, when the doors were locked, but they were often out much later. Jeremy Savage had a room on the ground floor, with conveniently large windows, which became a popular way in to hall after hours.

One night Geoff was creeping home late and was lurking in the bushes until the coast was clear when he was found by the duty warden. 'Hamilton! How come I find you hiding in the bushes?' Geoff replied, 'Because I didn't hear you coming, sir!' He was gated for that.

Geoff and Tony were also involved in many of the pranks that went on at college. At the time the name of the principal was Ben Harvey and Benskins was a local beer much favoured by the students. One night, they hijacked a hot-dog stand from Chelmsford, towed it back to college, deposited it on the front lawn, and then wrote 'Ben's Inn' in the style of the beer bottle label in fertilizer underneath it. Christopher Wagstaff, now Archdeacon of Gloucester Cathedral, was on the same horticulture course as Geoff and remembers the time they hijacked a workman's hut and set up their own road diversion right outside the gates of the college. And there was the occasion when the students tackled the car belonging to one of the lecturers who never cleaned it. They cleaned and polished one half of it immaculately, and left the other half in its usual filthy state.

Cars featured prominently in the college pranks. A new dining-hall had just been built with huge, floor-to-ceiling glass windows set in wooden frames. One night the Hamiltons and friends carefully unscrewed one of these huge window frames and lifted it to one side while they pushed another lecturer's car inside the dining-hall and then carefully replaced the window frame. In the morning when the staff came down for breakfast, there was the car in the middle of the dining-hall, and they couldn't work out how on earth it had got in there. It certainly couldn't have gone through the door.

Another lecturer who owned a car didn't get off quite so lightly, as Geoff often told Nick, who followed his father to Writtle and who now runs Barnsdale Plants and Gardens. 'Apparently this lecturer, who was also a warden of a hall of residence, came in one day in a particularly bad mood and was taking it out on everybody. So that night, they decided to hoist his car on to the roof, which was about 60 feet high. It was taken to bits and every part was hoisted up there by ropes and pulleys, where it was carefully reassembled. Next morning, this guy came tootling into college and there was his car up on the roof. They had to get a crane to get it down, and they never did find out who was responsible. But they know now!'

John Sales, who has only recently retired after 25 years as Head of Gardens for the National Trust, was a new junior lecturer at Writtle at the time. 'I must say that was one of the very best rag stunts I ever saw. Like Geoff, most of the students in that group had done national service and so were more grown up than those who came later straight from school. Then the pranks got rather more silly.'

John Sales came more or less straight from Kew, where he trained in horticulture, with no teacher training or experience at all, to teach a course in what was then called decorative horticulture. 'It was a minority subject. Most of the time was devoted to fruit and vegetable growing and glasshouse crops. Geoff, who was in his second year, wasn't particularly interested in my subject. He wanted to be a nurseryman, I remember. But they were a very good-humoured bunch and were kind to me on the whole.' Even so, he was subjected to the odd jape. 'Mine was the last lecture on a Friday afternoon, and they had got the message that I was going to carry on to the bitter end, and not let them out five minutes early. So one day they hid an alarm clock under the lectern, which went off at five to five. On another occasion – it was my birthday – suddenly all the lights went out and someone came in with a cake blazing with candles. There was also a lot of gentle ribbing emanating from the back of the room where Geoff always sat!'

But Geoff and his fellow students were in such awe of some lecturers that they didn't dare fool around. Monica Griffiths (now Meeneghan), who was on Geoff's course, remembers one incident in a practical glasshouse lecture. 'Ian Lambert, the senior lecturer in commercial horticulture, was rather quick-tempered, and we all trod very carefully with him. He'd usually come in, start dictating and that would be that. There was no question of discussion. One day in a lecture on chrysanthemums, I think it was, Geoff took him up on a point and started to argue hard with him. We all sat there with bated breath, waiting for the wrath to descend, but it didn't. Mr Lambert took it and argued back, and they were still hard at it when the lecture time was over and the rest of us quietly left!'

Over 20 years later, Geoff encountered Ian Lambert again. Nick recalls Geoff taking him to a show when he was about 17 at which Writtle had a stand. 'Ian Lambert was on the stand and I was trying to tell him that I was interested in going to horticultural college, but the old man kept on interrupting, until Ian Lambert said, "Geoff! Go and sit on that chair over there and be quiet!" And meek as a lamb, Geoff did as he was told.'

Ian Lambert, now retired from teaching, remembers Geoff with affection. 'He was a keen and natural learner and always a very nice fellow. He had a ready smile, and a good sense of humour. I was very firm sometimes in lectures, but I also knew when to relax a little and engage in a sensible discussion, and Geoff was one of the students with whom you could do that. He was clearly a keen horticulturist then, and that stayed with him. It always amused me when I watched him on television to see that he had remembered my insistence on adding organic matter and grit for aeration!'

For their twenty-first birthdays, Cyril bought Geoff and Tony a car, a 1936 Morris 8E series, which cost £15 and which, Tony says, was more collapsible than convertible. He gave them pocket money of 10 shillings a week each – that's 50p – and they used to run the car on that, though they remember both of them on a Friday some-times having to borrow a halfpenny to buy a cup of coffee before they went home and got their next ten bob. Geoff and Tony really loved that car and lavished time and effort on it, repainting it by hand several times, rebuilding the engine, and doing running repairs with the same ingenuity, economy and commitment to recycling that was to be Geoff's hallmark later on. 'One of the inside wheel arches was rusting away, so we decided we needed to do something about it. Obviously, we couldn't afford to have it welded, so we decided to cut out the affected part and bolt another piece of metal in its place. So we went round to the same sweet shop where we had once tried to buy sweets with Rosie's grocery tokens and pinched a metal sign that had "R. White's Lemonade" painted on it. We cut it up and bolted it into place, and we were so proud of our handiwork that we didn't put the carpet back over it.'

They used the car a lot together, but also separately when the need arose. 'I was driving in it one night,' Tony recalls, 'when I broke down at the top of Stamford Hill, so I rang Geoff and asked if he'd borrow Cyril's car and come and tow me home. So out he came, but the problem was first that the tow-rope was too short and second that Geoff insisted on driving home at 40 miles an hour. That was the top speed our car would do anyway, and driving down Stamford Hill, which was cobbled in those days, meant the car was bouncing about all over the road. I was banging on the hooter trying to get him to slow down, but all I got back was a cheery wave and he kept on going. When we finally got home I was furious. I said, "You bloody idiot, you nearly killed me!" He just grinned and said, "Well, I didn't, did I?"'

Despite all their efforts, the car became increasingly unreliable and kept catching fire. 'The old man used to tell us,' Nick said, 'that they thought if they just leapt out and left it to burn, then Cyril would have to buy them another car. But every time it caught fire, it was either just as they got home or just as they got back to college, so they couldn't leave it to burn. But one day it caught fire between the two places, so they jumped out and hid in the bushes, planning to watch it go up in smoke. Just then some bloke pulled up with his newly acquired fire-extinguisher and put out the blaze for them. You can just imagine the look on their faces!'

While Tony was happily settled with Christina, who was to be his first wife, Geoff had been playing the field, with a plentiful supply of girl friends. But in 1958 he went to a party in Pinner, north-west of London, given by a college friend and his sister, Joan. One of the other guests was a friend of Joan's, a very beautiful 22-year-old French woman called Colette Joulin. 'My first impression of Geoffrey was that he was a bit English – his hair was everywhere – and I suppose I thought he was handsome. I was a very shy person then. I have three sisters, and I went to school with only girls, so I wasn't really used to men.' Even so, when Geoff wrote to her care of Joan, asking if she would like to go out one evening, she accepted. The first date was memorable but for the wrong reasons. 'We went out for a meal, but I had a bad stomach and so we had to stop at every other café so that I could go to the loo!' But they survived the first date and Geoff was smitten. Richard Reed remembers that once he had met Colette, Geoff's mind was even less on his work than it had been before.

Geoff graduated in the summer of 1959, and finding a job became a top priority because he was taking on responsibilities. He and Colette were to be married in England at St Pancras Register Office on 14 December 1959 and in France at Colette's local church in St-Mandé, near Paris, one week later, on 21 December.

CHAPTER THREE

FAMILY MAN

After graduating from college, Geoff started work in commercial horticulture – back to the tomatoes for a short time, then a spell with Jack Allison, his old nurseryman friend who grew a wide range of other plants as well as tomatoes. But he realized that what he had enjoyed most of all was landscaping so, in 1960, rather bravely, he set up a landscaping business of his own based at his home in Wormley, a village very close to Broxbourne, where he and Colette had settled. He also rented a small piece of land around the corner, from a Mrs Hamilton coincidentally, on which to start a small nursery, growing the plants for his business.

As he told Radio Leicester in 1995, there was nothing he enjoyed more than building new gardens. 'That really is a great pleasure for me, and finding ways round the problems you come across really is a bit of a challenge. I love a nice bit of weedy old ground with brambles and goodness knows what. That really is a clean canvas to me, and you can do something very creative on it, and I love that.'

While Geoff had undoubtedly inherited his father's work ethic and put in very long hours, he hadn't inherited Cyril's head for business, nor was he interested in that side of the work. Since he enjoyed making gardens so much, he would often spend more time on a job than he had budgeted for, and so would come away at the end of it without much of a profit, or indeed sometimes even at a loss. According to Martin Frost, who worked for Geoff in those days, part of the problem was that he was a perfectionist. 'Everything had to be done absolutely right. I mean, turf was laid immaculately and when he'd finished it would look as though it had been there for ages.'

Not all of Geoff's employees at that time were that adept at laying turf, though. John Mold, who had known Geoff briefly in his scouting days, recalls working for him and laying turf in a garden they were doing in New Road, Broxbourne. 'I do remember Geoff shouting at me, "No, no, green side up!"' Tony remembers John as the archetypal 'man in the wrong job', and he abandoned horticuture for a job in the City, then emigrated to Canada, where he is now vice president of the Hong Kong Bank of Canada.

Tony believes that Geoff really wasn't interested in being a businessman or in making lots of money, and therefore missed many opportunities. There was the time when Geoff went to quote for a job in London. It was a very large house and the people were clearly very wealthy, but it was only a small job, worth about £90, and since Geoff didn't really want all the hassle of driving into London every day for such a small job he decided to quote such a ridiculous amount of money that they couldn't possibly accept it. So he quoted £900, and the people said 'Fine'. It was perhaps the first time he made proper money out of a job.

Another client of Geoff's was a big-time gambler, Martin Frost recalls. One Friday, after the man had given Geoff part-payment for the job in cash with which he was going to pay the wages, he persuaded Geoff to go along to a casino with him. 'Geoff, ever the adventurer, put the whole lot down on the table, and luckily he won. So we did get paid that night, but it was a close call! He didn't tell us about it until much later – several years later, in fact!'

Geoff was very good with customers, Martin Frost remembers, usually able to persuade them round to his way of thinking, and a very good man to work for. He was generous in allowing Martin free use of the van out of working hours and was not given to issuing orders. 'He would also say what he wanted to do and ask whether we thought it was possible. He was great fun – we saw each other a lot socially too – and an all-round good guy.'

Making sure that the money he was owed came in reasonably promptly was clearly important – cash flow is a major part of running any business successfully. But asking for money was something Geoff never enjoyed. On one occasion he had done a garden for a very smart house in Chelsea and had to drive in from Wormley to collect his fees. When he knocked on the door, a maid answered and said that her employers were out, although their car was parked outside. So he drove all the way home without his money. A few days later he went again, and this time the maid said that the mistress of the house was in the bath. Geoff said, 'Well, get her out of the bath then!', which she did. The woman wasn't pleased. 'Well, Mr Hamilton, I was going to recommend you to all my friends, but I'm not sure that I'm going to now.' Geoff bristled at this and said, 'If all your friends are like you, then frankly (drawing on the most famous line from *Gone with the Wind*) I don't give a damn!' Then he took his money and marched into the sunset. 'He was so frustrated by her behaviour,' Chris, his youngest son, says, 'that he just flipped, but as a businessman it wasn't a good thing to do.'

Landscaping was a hard way to make a living, and the first time Geoff ever got hold of £100 in a lump sum he went home with it in his hand and with a whoop of delight threw it all up in the air. The notes fluttered down the back of the sofa and behind pictures and furniture – only to be rediscovered gradually as the months went by. But he did make a go of the business, which did well until the winter of 1963. 'That was the worst winter I have ever known,' Geoff told Radio Leicester. 'They say that when you work on the land you get used to bad weather and shrug your shoulders and say, "Well, there's always next year." But '63 was *bad*. There were three months when there was snow on the ground and if you're a landscape gardener and there's snow on the ground, there is nothing you can do. I was still paying everybody – that's my conscience! – and it virtually bankrupted me. It was a very traumatic experience, and I really do sympathize now with people who are in this situation because of recession or other circumstances that are no fault of their own.'

The business staggered on for a few more years until 1967, but it was a real struggle and money was always scarce, a constant source of anxiety since by now there were three more mouths to feed. Stephen was born in January 1961, Nicholas (Nick) in April 1962 and Christopher (Chris) in January 1964. Not that they were aware of the problems Geoff was facing, and all recall their childhood as a very happy time.

Their first memories of their father – 'the old man', as they all call him – are very different. Stephen, now a garden photographer who worked very closely with Geoff on his books and magazine articles, remembers sitting on his father's knee when he was about four while Geoff did the *Guardian* crossword. 'He'd give me a clue and I'd say, "No, I don't know that one." Then he'd tell me the answer and explain it to me and I'd go, "Oh, right." He'd say, "You still don't get it, do you?" "Well, no." As if at four I would!'

Geoff loved words. He was brilliant at crosswords and could do them in record time; he loved puns and anagrams and any kind of wordplay. The boys all had nicknames, for example. Stephen was Step Hen, Nick was Tin Bum (nickle arse) and Chris was Loloff from his first attempts to say his own name, or Postie from someone else naming him Christie Postie, or later Christoff. Other friends and relatives had nicknames too – though not always to their faces. A relative called Kit was always referred to as Auntie Kitbag, and Geoff named another called Lucy 'LucyLastic'. 'I remember his face one day,' says Chris, 'when I said in all innocence in front of her, "Is LucyLastic staying for tea?"'

Nick's first clear memory involving his father is of being sick in the car, an old Austin 1300 that Geoff drove when he had the landscape gardening business. 'I suffered terribly from car sickness as a kid, and I can remember I used to be sick over the old man's tools that he kept in the well behind the front seat. He always used to make me clean the tools afterwards – the drill in particular still haunts me. I thought it was very unfair, but I suppose he thought that if I had to clean it up I wouldn't be sick next time. But I always was.'

For Chris, who started out as a potter and is now head of the art department in a comprehensive school, his earliest memory is of Geoff inadvertently putting him off gardening for life. 'I had watered a plant through its leaves, and he came out and said, very nicely, "No, you don't do it that way. You water the soil around the plant." And I thought, this is too difficult for me, too much like hard work. Later on he was always trying to get me into gardening, telling me how interesting it was to watch plants grow, but I always thought it was boring. The closest we got was when I was working as a potter and I said that I'd get into gardening if he had a go at pottery, and he said "No, too boring," so that was that.'

They all agree that although Geoff, like most fathers of his generation, wasn't around that much when they were small – self-employed landscapers work as long as it stays light – when he was there he was great fun. 'The child in him never grew up,' Nick says, 'something he inherited from Cyril, and so when he was with us that side of him would come out. He wasn't the sort of dad who'd come in from work and just want to sit down and be left alone for half an hour. He enjoyed being with us and behaved like he was our age.' There were monster-chasing games and tickling games – 'You were offered Rapid Death or Slow Lingering Death, which basically involved differing strengths and durations of tickling' – and rituals.

They used to go camping in Cornwall when the boys were small, basically because Geoff and Colette had no money for more sophisticated holidays, and, besides, Geoff loved roughing it in the country-side. As Nick says, he was never happier in later life than when there was a power cut at Barnsdale, and he could get the primus stove out. 'The three of us would be tucked up in our sleeping-bags in the tent,' Chris remembers, 'and he'd say, "Right, now I don't want to hear a peep out of you!" and as he left we'd all go "Peep!" and he'd turn round and say, "Right, now I don't want to hear another peep out of you!" and it would go on like that for hours.'

Whenever they were driving and passed a town or village with 'ham' at the end of its name, Geoff would parody the old Peter Sellers record 'Bal-ham, Gateway to the South'. And for a while, whenever one of the boys got in his way, he would say in a Scottish accent, 'Hoots mon! Get oot ma wa'. Who d'ya think y'are!' 'He loved doing a Scottish accent even though he was pretty terrible at it,' Chris says. 'One day he was in a pub up there and said to the barman, "I'll have a wee dram, if you please," then turned to the bloke standing next to him at the bar and said, "It's terrible. Whenever I'm in Scotland, I just can't resist doing the accent. I suppose one day someone's going to hit me!" And the guy said, "Aye, and it cud be me!"'

Talking in silly voices was also a great family habit. Chris recalls a Monty Python sketch involving two characters on the telephone endlessly saying 'Hello' to each other in the same very silly voice. 'One day the old man was in the office when the phone rang and the voice at the other end said "Hello", so he said "Hello" in the same silly voice, and then the other man said "Oh hello, Mr Hamilton, I'm ringing about..." whatever it was. The old man had to carry on speaking in the silly voice until he could very gradually revert to his own.'

Geoff loved family sayings, passing on to his children things his parents used to say to him when he was a boy. ' "Don't be a meddle-some Mattie" was one of them,' Stephen remembers, 'and if Rosie

ever spilt something or knocked something over, she'd say to whoever was nearest, "That's thinking of you, that is!" And only a few
years ago, when we were working on *First Time Garden*, he asked me
if a fence post was straight and I said, "Near enough." He came back
with, "Near enough's not good enough, as my old dad used to say." '

And Geoff invented some of his own too. When the boys were
kids and they asked him how to do something, he'd repeat it back to
them in a silly voice. 'Ooh, I don't know, Daddy. How do I make this
work, Daddy?' 'But when he first got his computer, he didn't have a
clue how to operate it. Not a clue. It would be, "Stephen, tell me
again, how do I back the work up?" I'd do it to him in the same silly
voice. "Ooh, Stephen. How do I back it up, Stephen?" And he loved
it because he knew that tradition was being carried on. He loved all
the old family stuff, the stories and the sayings. It was almost as
though he thought of the Hamiltons as a dynasty.'

Geoff certainly used to impress on the boys the value of family.
'He was always saying to us when we were trying to kill each other,
"Your brothers are your brothers and nothing will ever change that.
You'll be glad you've got them when you're 20." And I used to
think, "Oh, yeah? Never! I hate them!" But it did stick in the end,
and I do think the way we were brought up has meant we have
stuck together as brothers.'

Geoff also had enormous loyalty to wider family, too, like the time
a cousin who was a builder ran into hard times when the building
industry virtually collapsed during the recession. He invited him to
come to Barnsdale and found all sorts of work for him to do. Tony
asked Geoff at the time if he could really afford all this. He was surprised by the question. 'He's family, boy!' was Geoff's reply.

Geoff was also a great one for making simple things into an event,
like the naming of the stray cat that came one day and stayed. 'I can
see the old man now,' says Chris, 'sitting on a chair the wrong way
round with the cat in front of him, and going through lists of names

of Russian playwrights and politicians. The cat just sat there, unmoving, until he said "Pushkin", which got a definite response, so Pushkin it became.'

Christmas was always very special, with rituals that Stephen still carries on with his two daughters. 'All the presents were under the tree, and usually you got one really good present and lots of little things as well. There were always clues on the big presents, usually so obscure that you couldn't possibly guess them, but that was half the fun. One year, the other two had got their big present, but I hadn't had mine. On the tree, though, there was a little note saying "Follow me," with a thread attached. I followed the thread and it went all over the house – up the stairs, through the bedrooms and the bathroom, out into the garden and back in again. Eventually, there under the stairs was a new bike. It was absolutely fantastic. One of the best moments of my life, I'd say. It must have taken him ages, and how he did it I really don't know because we didn't go to sleep until late with excitement and we were awake again at 3 a.m. But I did the same thing when my elder daughter Eddie got her new bike and it was not easy!'

Every Christmas Eve Geoff would read to them all from *A Christmas Carol* and he read extremely well, as Stephen remembers with great pleasure. 'He made it all so real that we really used to look forward to it every year – me more than my brothers, perhaps, because I loved reading so much, something that he was very pleased about. He made such a brilliant choice of books for me when I was small, all the children's classics he felt I should read, and I am extremely grateful to him for that.'

While the child in Geoff made him great fun as a father, there were times when it should have been suppressed and wasn't. Chris remembers an occasion when they were playing in the garden on their climbing frame and Nick persuaded him to shout out something rude. 'I don't remember what, precisely, but it had the word nude in it. My mother was absolutely furious and hauled us all in from the garden. "Go on. Tell your father what you just said. Go on, tell him!" I could already see that the old man was desperately trying not to laugh, and when I repeated it he just collapsed in fits. I still got sent to bed, though.'

When Geoff and Colette went out for the evening, Geoff's grandmother Ally would often babysit. 'As they left,' recalls Stephen, 'the old man would say, "Now I want them in bed by 8 o'clock," and Ally would say, "Right-oh, Geoff!" But she loved wrestling, so she'd have us all in our vests and shorts, having tag-wrestling matches in the sitting-room, me against the two younger ones, until quite late. We'd wait until we heard the car draw up outside, then belt up the stairs. I'd put the light on for a second to get Chris and Nick into bed, switch it off and dive into my bed. Then we'd hear his steps on the stairs. "Are you asleep?" and we never answered. Years later, he told me that they used to wait outside until they saw the light go on and off again and then come in! He always told Ally off for letting us stay up, but it never stopped her.'

Although they were rarely smacked, Stephen remembers being frightened of Geoff's anger. 'He was quite terrifying when he was cross. Of course, it was mainly bluster, but terrifying none the less. When I was about five, I decided my bike needed a paint job, so I took the wheels off and brought it into the front room. I put some newspapers down on the dark brown carpet – this was the mid-1960s – and got a tin of white gloss. There I was painting away and I inadvertently knocked the paint over on to the carpet. I thought, oh, my God, I'm dead. He'll go bananas. So logic dictated that the best thing to do would be to paint the whole carpet with white gloss, then no one would know. So there I was busily painting the whole carpet when he walked in...' And then there was the time when the boys were playing football in the garden and Stephen kicked it right through the dining-room window. 'He wasn't best pleased, and went off to the glazier, got a new piece of glass and put it in. And then, blow me, if ten minutes later I didn't kick the ball straight through the same window. I was expecting the wrath to descend, but he just replaced the glass again and said, "No more football!"'

Worse in some ways, Stephen remembers, were the reasonable talkings-to, which were Geoff's way of dealing with bad behaviour later. One day he had been playing in the woods with a friend when they came across a camp someone had made and in it was a copy of *Playboy*. 'We thought this was fantastic, Adrian and I, so we tore it in half, and had half each. I put my half down the front of my shorts, and as I walked in through the back garden the old man happened to be standing looking out of the dining-room window. I could already feel the pages starting to slip, and I thought, "I can't let the old man see these," so I dived into the shed and hid the pictures in there. Then he said, "Where have you been?" "Playing with Adrian." "No, I mean just now." "Well, in the shed." "What for?" "Er ... nothing." All I could do was deny! He said, "Wait there," and within two seconds he was back with the pictures. "What are these then?" "Dunno." Then he decided to give me The Talk. "It's all perfectly natural and normal." I had to sit through the whole sexual history of man since time began, although, of course, I knew it already. Appalling it was, so embarrassing. I'll never forget it!'

Perhaps because of his own upbringing, and the fact that he didn't have any money to spare, it was very important to Geoff that his sons appreciated what they had and were grateful. For that reason, he was not amused when they celebrated Easter by crucifying the Action Man they'd been given only the previous Christmas on the garden fence, with liberal applications of red paint and nails. Chris remembers the time Geoff bought him a little fishing-rod, and he was standing on Cyril's motor-boat fishing in the river. 'I managed to fall in, and in the process dropped my rod. I scrambled up on to the boat dripping wet, and the old man said, "Where's your rod?" I said, "I dropped it." "Well," he said, "you'd better go and get it then," and pushed me back in!'

Pocket money – sixpence a week – had to be earned, Stephen remembers, although the work done for it varied from week to week. 'One week I had to move a whole stack of bags of compost from one place to another – took me all day and I'm sure it didn't really need doing. Yet another week, all I had to do was clean the shoes. But it was important to him that we did something – you didn't get anything for nothing.'

Geoff couldn't bear them wasting food, either, even if it were something he had grown himself. One day Stephen decided to make a stand over spinach, which he loathed (and still does). 'He said that I would have to sit there until I ate it, but I had decided this was it and I wasn't going to eat it whatever he said or did. So I sat at the table with the spinach in front of me for about an hour after everyone else had finished, and then he said, "Right, upstairs to your room with it, and stay there. I was going to take you all to the fair this afternoon, but if you haven't eaten it by the time I come up, then you won't be going." And he never made threats without carrying them out, so I thought, OK, so I won't be going to the fair, then. When he came up to my room an hour or two later, the spinach was still there on the plate and I said, "I'm not going to eat it." He said, "All right," and off we went to the fair. He just wanted to make sure I really meant it.'

Whenever a misdemeanour had been committed, Geoff would line the three boys in descending order of height and grill them. 'He always worked on the assumption that it was me,' Stephen remembers, 'because usually it was. We used to have a family pack of Kit-Kats as a treat sometimes – five in a pack, so one for each of us. One day, having wolfed mine down in one go as usual, in a moment of madness I ate the old man's too. So there was the usual Spanish Inquisition. "Come on, Stephen, I know it was you!" I cried and said, "It's not fair, you always blame me." And for once he let it go. Later – 25 years later, I didn't dare mention it before – I told him that I'd had his Kit-Kat. "I knew it!" he said. I never let him forget it. That was one of the few things I ever got away with.'

Apart from work and his family, the other major interest in Geoff's life at this time was rowing. Having coxed and started rowing with Broxbourne Rowing Club on the River Lea when he was still at school, he'd had no opportunity to carry on in the RAF or at college. When he settled back in Wormley, near Broxbourne, in his early twenties, though, he took up the sport again, rowing with Tony in eights and fours and also sculling. In a sport where a good big 'un will almost always beat a good little 'un, Geoff's light, wiry build was always going to be a disadvantage, but what he lacked in physical strength he made up for in determination, and he did do well, winning a number of cups for sculling.

'"Energetic and enthusiastic" are the words that best describe Geoff as a rower,' says John Stoddart, a fellow member of Broxbourne Rowing Club and now Principal of Sheffield Hallam University. As a member at that time of the National Rowing Squad, he knows of what he speaks. 'He was well aware of his physical limitations, but he put in a hell of a lot of work on the water. He was very competitive, but he never got upset when he didn't win.' Except, that is, on one occasion, when he competed in the Boston Marathon, a long-distance handicap race. 'It's 36 miles,' Tony Hamilton says, 'and when you consider that the Boat Race is only a mile and a half, you can see that it would be pretty exhausting. You have to wear gloves and two pairs of underpants because you'd get blisters on your hands and backside. Anyway, Geoff did the fastest time, no question, but because there had been some sort of mix-up on someone else's timing, the other guy was awarded the race.'

Colette took the boys along to watch, and Nick remembers seeing Geoff go past, sculling with grim determination. 'He wound up with great blisters on his hands, and he was absolutely devastated because he knew that he had really won the race. That was the only time I ever saw him truly disappointed about anything, and I think after that he lost heart with rowing to a degree.'

When John Stoddart moved into the Broxbourne area in 1964, the rowing clubhouse had been burnt to the ground and was just a shell. He got to know Geoff very well, since they were both closely involved in raising the money to build a new clubhouse and equip it with boats, oars and a good bar – the essential ingredients for a successful oarsman.

Geoff was a very good officer of the club, whether as captain or secretary, efficient, loyal, and able to use his charm when necessary, as Shiner Pettifer, whose husband was taught to row by Geoff, and who became a good friend, recalls. 'One day, a rower had cut through the line of a fisherman, who was fishing from the river bank. The man was furious and came storming into the clubhouse ready to hit somebody. Geoff calmed him down, gave him a drink, and by the time the chap left, Geoff had got him to sign up as an associate member!'

Geoff's closest friend from rowing-club days, though, was John Stoddart. 'We both had young families of about the same age, so it was easy to go to regattas together, and that made for a strong social bond. We also enjoyed each other's company a lot, shared a similar sense of humour, and if I'm honest we both had a similar childlike – some would say childish – view of the world and a youthful irresponsibility, despite the real responsibilities we both had.'

Shiner Pettifer recalls an example of those youthful high spirits. 'They'd been to a regatta somewhere, and they both had their sculling boats on top of their cars – John Stoddart's was a rather smart estate car, and Geoff's was yet another of the beat-up Minis or some such that he always seemed to have. They were having some sort of a race, and at every set of traffic lights along the main street Stoddart would accelerate away first because he had the faster car.

The next thing we knew, there was this frantic beeping, and people standing back, stunned, as Geoff's Mini came driving up the pavement, got to the traffic lights before Stoddart and, when they changed, went roaring away in front!'

There were all kinds of pranks in rowing-club days, too, like the time when they had a very early start for a regatta and one oarsman overslept. Geoff and Tony and a few other friends went to his house, carefully lifted his bed with him in it still asleep, his bedside table, alarm clock and lamp, and put them all on the pavement outside. He was woken by early shoppers, passing by in bemused amazement.

Shiner Pettifer remembers Geoff with great affection, for the twinkle in his eye and for the scruffy old jumpers and hiking-boots he always wore. 'He came to stay with us one night, and he knew my husband had to get up very early to catch a plane, so he came in at dawn with two cups of tea wearing only the jumper, the boots and a pair of knickers.' She also remembers his fondness for jokes. 'Once, the local furniture shop in Hoddesdon High Street had a special offer – £100 off any new suite when you traded in the old one. I happened to be walking along the high street when Geoff grabbed me and said, "Colette has picked a suite she likes, and I want to check it out, so come in with me and pretend to be my wife." So in we went and sat on this suite, and Geoff was most solicitous. "Do you like it, darling? Is it comfortable?" Then he said to the salesman, "Now let me get this right. You will give me £100 off this suite if I part-exchange my old one?" "Yes, sir," the salesman said, "that is correct. Who is the manufacturer of your present suite?" and Geoff said, "I'm not entirely sure, but it does have Jaffa printed on every other plank of the seat!"'

Every summer, Colette would take the children off to France to stay with her family for a month, leaving Geoff behind. 'We used to have open house for rowers,' Shiner Pettifer says, 'and Geoff used to come and stay sometimes. We used to have great Sunday-night cockney teas, and there'd be competitions to see who could get the prawns peeled and the winkles out of their shells fastest. But then the night before Colette was due home with the boys, he'd dash in and ask us to come and help him clear up the house before she got back.'

Geoff and Colette lived close to the River Lea, and Colette would often take the boys for a walk in the field opposite the rowing club. When Geoff saw them on the other side of the river, he'd whistle, the three boys would strip off, jump into the water and swim across. Geoff would fish them out, dry them off and buy them a lemonade and some crisps while Colette walked the long way round.

The rowing club features prominently in the boys' memories of their childhood because they spent so much time there at weekends and in the holidays. There was, for example, the old dinghy with a hole in the bottom. 'The old man persuaded us that it would be great fun to row this thing out into the middle of the river – which we did with great difficulty – and then to stand there saluting while the boat sank slowly beneath us! Then we had to drag it all the way back to the bank again – under water.' Then there was the night of the rowing-club dinner when, most unusually, Geoff was dressed in hired black tie and dinner jacket. The boys, who were then very young, were playing outside, having been warned not to go too close to the water. 'I was playing on the slipway,' Nick recalls, 'which was covered in algae and was very slippery. Of course, I fell straight in. The old man saw me do it, came tearing out of the clubhouse and dived straight in to pull me out. I was taken to the changing-rooms, dried off and given a rugby shirt to put on, which was obviously miles too big for me and fell in folds round my feet. The old man was cross, but not overly cross. I just wish I'd been there on the Monday when he had to take the dinner jacket back to the shop, smelling of fetid river water!'

Geoff was always encouraging the boys to have a go at things – not forcing them or insisting, but just persuading them that it would be fun. He talked Nick into entering a swimming race across the river once. 'I didn't want to go in for it because the others were all older than me and would obviously beat me easily, but he said, "Just do your best." I came last by a mile, but I got a prize for coming last and I was chuffed to bits. He also persuaded me to have a go at coxing a boat – again, I wasn't keen. "Just do it!" he said. "It'll be good fun. Just try it once and see if you like it." So I had a go and hit the bank, and they never asked me again!'

Geoff enjoyed his rowing-club days, partly for the company and the very full social life but also because being out on the water, sculling on his own, was an escape from the problems he was having with his business. 'I knew he was struggling,' says John Stoddart, 'because he would sometimes talk to me about the problems he was facing, and at one stage I helped him out financially.'

By 1967 the business was in such trouble that there was really no alternative but to let it fold. With a family to support, Geoff had to find another way of making a living fast, and so he took whatever work he could find. He spent a little time doing garden design and consultancy work, but this was before the big gardening boom, and such work was very hard to find. But he was never the sort of person who could sit back and do nothing or draw benefit, so he took any-thing that was going, which was mainly work on the land. He even worked at carrot-topping for a while – a really dreary job, lifting carrots and slicing the leaves off – and his boys think that afterwards he was quite proud of having done it.

Eventually, as a last resort, in 1970, as Geoff told Radio Leicester, he took a job with Cyril. 'This was a moment of utter desperation, believe me, because my dad used to sell engineering materials. He was jolly good at it and made a very good living. So he gave me this job out of the kindness of his heart, and he gave me the best terri-tory for selling engineering materials in the country – Birmingham.'

Before he started work, Cyril decided that Geoff needed a bit of training, so he drove him up to a factory and told him to go in there and see what he could sell. Geoff duly did as he was told and began trying to sell parts for boilers and pipework to the maintenance engineer. After about ten minutes, the man said to Geoff, 'Do you know what we make here?' Geoff didn't know. 'We make candles – by hand.' Very embarrassed, Geoff went back out to the car, where Cyril was sitting with a smirk on his face because he knew what sort of factory it was. 'You've learnt lesson number one,' Cyril said when Geoff remonstrated with him. 'Always find out what your customer makes before you try to sell him anything!'

Despite that unpromising start, Geoff embarked on his sales career, but things didn't get any better. 'I was there for six months, and I didn't take a single order. Not one. Years later, I was rather proud of that record, but at the time, believe me, it was a disaster! Eventually, I decided that I was not cut out to be anything else but a gardener.

'What I haven't told you is that I believe there is some lady up there in the sky who looks down on me and says, "We gotta give this guy a break." And she looked down on me that day. I was doing this terrible job and it was a lovely sunny day and I was in the country going to Birmingham and I thought, It's such a lovely sunny day, I'll go the pretty way. So I drove the pretty way, and I saw, standing outside a gate, a pile of turf, a few boards, a barrow and a rake. And I looked at those things and I thought to myself, I have got to become a landscape gardener again. I have got to get back into it.

'I went into the very first garden centre I passed on the road and asked if I could borrow the trade papers. The chap lent one to me and in it was an advertisement for a piece of land that could be turned into a garden centre. It was a box number. It said, "A mile off the busy A6 in a thriving Midlands town." So I turned round, went back home, phoned the magazine and said, "Can you give me the phone number of this box number?" And they said, "No, we can't. That's what we have box numbers for." So I said, "At least would you do me the favour of giving the advertiser my phone number and asking him to phone me." I then got back in the car and drove up the A6 and went a mile off it on every road in the Midlands until I found this place – in Kettering – so that I could say to the man when he rang, "Yes, I'll have it." He agreed to let me rent it, and so I became the proud proprietor of a small garden centre in Kettering.' It was a plot of land with a single-storey building on it and a few sheds, which Geoff called the Hamilton Garden Centre. The boys remember the first day, in 1971, when Geoff drove proudly home in the van with the name painted on the side.

'He lined us all up in descending height as usual,' Stephen recalls, 'and said, "Right, Christopher, there you are!" And out of the back of the van came a brand-new bike for Christopher. Then it was Nick's turn – a brand-new bike came out of the back of the van for Nick. Then he turned to me and said, "Well, Stephen, you've already got a bike..." and, indeed, I was the only one of us who did have a bike then "... so here's a new saddlebag to go on it!" I was crushed, absolutely crushed, and was trying desperately hard to be grateful. And he left me like that for ages, and then said, "Oh, all right then. Here's a new bike to go with it!" That was typical of him. I mean, he'd planned the whole thing. He'd deliberately bought the separate saddlebag just so he could pull that joke on me!'

The well-known plantswoman Valerie Finnis, who lives in Kettering, met Geoff soon after he had opened the garden centre. 'My late husband (Sir David Scott) and I used to propagate hundreds of plants for our open days under the National Gardens Scheme and we always had a surplus, so we wondered whether we might find a nursery locally to buy them from us. So, very shyly, I went into Geoff's garden centre and asked if he would like to buy these plants, which he did. After that he used to drive over quite often to buy more plants from us, and it seemed to me that he always worked so hard. I realized that the business wasn't doing too well, and towards the end his parents used to be serving in the shop to help out. As far as I know, Geoff was working on people's gardens, and in fact I believe there are still several Geoff Hamilton gardens in London Road in Kettering which have a historical interest now.'

Again, although Geoff had clearly inherited his father's work ethic and worked extremely hard, he lacked the head for business that had made Cyril succeed. Tony, on the other hand, had by this time moved out of farming into management, and in the early days of the garden centre he used to spend the weekends helping Geoff, not only by working in the garden centre but also by doing his books and giving him what advice he could. As Geoff told the *Daily Mail* in 1996, 'One day Tone said to me, "OK, where's your budget?" And I said, "Budget? What budget?" And that about sums it up. I had the worst thing a businessman could have, Tone told me, and that was optimism. It's no good saying I know this will work: in business you've got to know why it will work. Tone knows and I don't.'

During this time, Tony was suddenly taken ill with a brain haemorrhage and was unconscious in the neurological unit of Derby Hospital for two weeks. 'I received a great deal of support from Geoff during that time. Although I was unconscious, the neurologist said it would be helpful if someone talked to me, so Geoff used to come every night, sit by my bed and talk to me. He said afterwards it was the most difficult thing, having to keep talking to someone who was completely ignoring him! He said he lost count of the number of times he said to me, "When this is all over, Tone, we'll go down to the pub for a pint!" – anything, however banal, just to keep the flow of chat going.'

Tony has no memories of that time, but he does remember waking up in the Leicester Royal Infirmary, to which he was later transferred, with a nurse leaning over him and saying, 'My word, it's good to have you back, Mr Hamilton.' 'Back?' said Tony. 'Where have I been?' Then she told him he'd been unconscious for two weeks, and his first thought was what people always say when they're trying to give up smoking – the first two weeks are the most difficult. Immediately, he thought, my goodness, I've just got it for free. So there and then he gave up and has never smoked since.

While he was recovering he was able to spend more time with Geoff at the garden centre and got to see his business practices at first hand. Tony believes that part of the problem was that Geoff was a perfectionist and wanted to have the widest possible range of exotic trees and shrubs for sale. So he used to buy in all kinds of plants that nobody wanted to buy. Tony used to say to him, 'Look, you need to work out what it is that people are buying, then buy in those things and don't worry about the rest.' But he wouldn't have it. Geoff believed earnestly that people should be able to choose from the very best. This was probably the start of his desire to communicate his own enthusiasm to others. His downfall was that he was not hard-headed enough to realize that what most of his customers really wanted was exactly what their neighbours had.

When Geoff started the garden centre, Nick discovered the passion for growing plants that is still with him today and, when he was nine and ten, he spent a lot of time there with his father. He believes that, once again, Geoff's love for what he was doing led to his downfall. 'What he should really have had was a nursery, not a garden centre, because, although he did buy some stock in, he grew most of the plants himself, which was very unusual for a garden centre, unless it's part of a big chain. That's what he loved doing most – growing plants, and telling customers all about them. Most garden centres these days are really supermarkets for sundries, furniture, lawn mowers and so on, on which they make far more profit. Plants seem to come very low on their list of priorities, but he wasn't interested in selling garden sundries. Plants were his passion, and the time and space he devoted to them in our garden centre was enormous.'

Tony agrees. 'When you run a garden centre you are basically a shopkeeper, and he just didn't like being a shopkeeper. He didn't like the fact that he had to go round with a feather duster and dust all the stock, so he didn't do it and the place always looked terrible. What he did extremely well, though, was to advise people, and they would stream in to get Geoff's advice, spend half a day talking to him about what they should do in their gardens and not spend any money. He even used to go off to their gardens with them to show them what to do, because that's what he really wanted to be doing. It was only later that he found the way to do it.'

Cor van Hage, who has turned the small nursery he started in Broxbourne in the 1950s in to a multimillion-pound garden centre success, was very surprised that Geoff didn't make a go of it. 'Geoff was always a very hard worker. He was certainly brainy enough, he knew enough and he was a very good salesman. But I think running a successful business is a combination of common sense, ambition and hard work, and I don't know whether he was ambitious enough or whether he realized just how much hard work is required to build a business. I said something to him about it a year or two after it had collapsed. I told him I was surprised because he had been to the best school in the country – me! He joked back that if he hadn't worked for me he wouldn't be in this mess now! But I got the feeling he didn't want to talk about it seriously, so I let it go.'

At the time when the business was on the point of collapse in 1973, another blow hit the family. Geoff and Colette separated and Geoff moved out. For the boys, this came as a total shock. 'They had their arguments,' Nick, who was nearly 11 at the time, recalls, 'but never in front of us children, so the decision to split came as a complete bolt from the blue.' Stephen believes the basic problem was that his parents just grew apart, with different interests and different values. 'When I was much older, the old man said to me that his greatest regret was the fact that he and my mother had split up, by which he meant the fact that it had been impossible for them to stay together. He was a great believer in the value of family, because his own childhood had been so happy, and he deeply regretted that he was not able to provide the same for his own children.'

It was a painful time for everybody, but Geoff worked hard to maintain a good relationship with the boys, seeing them every week-end – or almost every weekend. 'Occasionally, he didn't turn up,' Nick recalls, 'but we knew that he had the worst memory in the world, and so, though it may sound odd, we never felt aggrieved by it and, because of the relationship we had with him, it really didn't matter. We'd wait for a bit and then we'd say, "Doesn't look as though he's coming," and go off to play quite happily. Next time we saw him, he'd usually have planned something special for us.'

One of Geoff's little quirks, which his boys still smile about, was his habit of always doing his Christmas shopping at 5 p.m. on Christmas Eve. Even so, they were rather startled when he arrived one Christmas morning to drop off their presents – a sock full of money each. He claimed that he hadn't forgotten to go shopping and this was what he'd planned. What he'd been doing when he got home from work every night was to dump all his loose change in a drawer. So when he'd missed the shops on Christmas Eve, he'd found three clean socks and scooped handfuls of money out of this drawer to fill them up. When the boys emptied them out and started count-ing, they found, to their delight, that they each had about £30, which was a lot of money in the mid-1970s.

While Geoff had been running the garden centre, he had also started writing the odd freelance gardening article. By a lucky coinci-dence, the man from whom he had rented the land for the garden centre in Kettering – almost certainly John Parker, although we have been unable to trace him – turned out to be the editor of *Garden News*, the weekly gardening magazine based in Peterborough. He was a rowing man, too, and so they became good friends, and eventually he asked Geoff if he'd like to try to write something for the magazine.

'Well, I saw this as a great opportunity because I had always been good at English at school, so I thought I'm bound to be a great success here. So I sat there and wrote 500 words of the best gardening copy you have ever seen in your life. It took me three weeks, and I polished it and polished it until it was absolutely perfect. Then I took it down and showed it to him and he said, "God, we can't use this!" So I said to him, "Rewrite it and show me what I've got to do." He rewrote it, and I don't think I've looked back since.'

Although he didn't know it at the time, Geoff had found the perfect career – a chance to combine his passion for making gardens, for growing plants and for communicating that passion to as many people as possible.

CHAPTER FOUR

STARTING OVER

At the time Geoff was starting to write the odd freelance article for *Garden News*, the technical editor was Geoff Amos, who later featured on Central TV's *Gardening Time* for many years and also on Radio Leicester until his recent retirement.

'It was part of my job to deal with freelance articles that people sent in, and Geoff Hamilton's were among them. I knew of him, and knew that he had a small garden centre in Kettering that wasn't doing too well, so I went to see him and took the piece with me. I told him, "This is all right – it's good gardening, but it's four times too long and it's not written in the sort of language *Garden News* readers will understand. We never use long words where short ones will do." Once it was pointed out to him, he knew in a minute what was wanted. He was very quick on the uptake, was Geoff.'

When Geoff was asked by Radio Leicester's John Florence what was the first, most important lesson he learnt about journalism, he replied, 'The problem with writing is the discipline. You simply cannot say, "I don't feel like it today, I'll do it tomorrow," because if you do you are on the rocky road to perdition and you'll miss your deadline. The Rule No. 1 of journalism, which I was taught on my very first day, is *never mind what the copy's like so long as it's there on time*.'

That would have amused Frank Ward, the editor of *Garden News* at that time. 'He was late with copy almost every week! I was always on the phone chasing him up, and he always had some feeble excuse. We used to exchange insults with great relish, and indeed when Geoff joined the staff we made up a crossword between us in which the answer to every clue was an insult!' Frank also shared Geoff's love of anagrams, and the anagram of Hamilton, 'Thin Loam', soon became his nickname in the office.

In 1973, the new editor of *Garden News*, Peter Peskett, received a phone call from Geoff saying he needed to see him urgently. They met that evening in a pub near Peterborough. 'Geoff explained that his business was in serious trouble, and since some of his creditors advertised in the paper, he felt that it might cause us embarrassment if he carried on writing for us and so would quite understand if we couldn't use him any more. I said that had nothing to do with us, and asked him what he was going to do next. When he said he didn't know, I offered him a staff job on the spot because I rated him so highly. There wasn't a vacancy as it happened, but I thought I'd just do it and square it with my publisher later!'

Initially, Tony says, Geoff was anxious that he might not be able to do it, but he settled down quickly and wrote some good articles, although there were a few bloomers. Tony recalls going into the newsagents early on in his days as a columnist and turning to his page. 'There in the middle of it was a black and white photograph of some weeds growing in his garden. What had happened apparently was that he found the piece wasn't big enough to fill the page and, rather than write more words, he'd searched through his photographs to find something to fit, and this was the only suitable picture he could find. Underneath it, as a caption, he had written, "Weeds are an abomination to the good gardener." I fell about laughing when I read this, and for ever more I used to creep up behind him in the dark recesses of the night and whisper, "Weeds are an abomination to the good gardener." When a man makes a juicy mistake – never let him forget it!'

His colleagues were more forgiving, and he soon established a reputation for being knowledgeable and helpful. 'There were quite a few people in the office who were journalists rather than gardeners,' Geoff Amos remembers, 'and he soon became the chap they would ask for advice, along with me.'

Geoff didn't spend all his time in the office, though. He and Geoff Amos spent some of their time reporting the big horticultural shows. 'We did a show at Harrogate once, and we were staying at the Swan. It was quite a smart place, and you had to wear a jacket and tie for dinner. Well, Geoff came down for dinner, dressed as usual in jeans and a checked shirt, with no tie of course, and they wouldn't let him in. So Geoff just turned round and disappeared to the pub!'

It was also part of Geoff's job to attend press conferences and, as with everything else Geoff did, they were an opportunity for a laugh as well as gathering useful material for the magazine. Frank Ward recalls a press conference one afternoon which was just about to start when a dowager gardening columnist came in very late and rather unsteadily. 'As she sat down she broke wind very noisily, at which Geoff stood up and applauded loudly, to the delight of the ribald gentlemen of the press.'

Geoff was also involved in the magazine's gardeners' question time sessions at garden centres and horticultural societies up and down the country, organized in association with Fisons. The man in charge of them was Roger Chown, from EMAP Publishing's promotions department. 'After the first 20 or so, it all got a bit boring. It was the same format each time – some questions, a promotional film that I was in charge of showing, and more questions – and often the same questions would come up time after time. Geoff was most certainly not someone who tolerated boredom, so as we were driving down to yet another of these sessions at a helicopter factory in Yeovil, Geoff said, "I tell you what – if I can make you laugh during the show, you buy all the booze tonight, and if you can make me laugh,

I'll do the buying." I thought I had the advantage because I was standing at the back of the hall ready to show the film, where the audience couldn't see me, but of course the panellists could. During the first question-and-answer session, I was doing everything I could think of to make Geoff laugh. I was pulling faces, sticking my finger up my nose, balancing on a chair… but got nothing out of Geoff at all. His face was like granite. So then I showed the film, and afterwards Geoff Amos, who was chairing the session, asked for the first question. A little old lady stood up and said, "I'd like to ask the panel why the leaves on my rubber plant keep turning yellow and dropping off." Geoff indicated to the chairman that he'd like to take the question, and then said, "Well, I think I can help you, madam, but first of all I need to know what variety of rubber plant it is. Is it a Durexica or a Gossamerus?" Nobody in the audience got it, but needless to say I bought the booze that night!'

In 1971 *Garden News* decided to build a garden at the Chelsea Flower Show, and Geoff, with his design and landscaping experience, was the ideal man to oversee the project. To help him build the garden, Geoff called on Martin Frost, his old employee from his landscaping days, and they did it between them with the help of just one labourer. 'It was quite a tricky design, lots of brick circles that had to be cut by hand, and one day I left my angle grinder at home. So I went to the local hardware shop, bought a club hammer and a brick bolster, and although Geoff teased me about it, it was so satisfying doing it that way that I just carried on.' His most vivid memory of that first Chelsea garden, though, is of Geoff walking and talking in animated fashion, stepping backwards into the pond and stepping out again, still talking without missing a beat.

The following year Geoff had a very radical idea for a garden at Chelsea. It was called the Garden of the Future – and was basically a large plastic dome, blown up with hot air provided by a fan driven by a little two-stroke motor. 'The one problem with it,' Roger

Chown recalls, 'was that the fuel tank was quite small and would run for only four hours at a time. So what we had to do was organize a rota system. We'd fill the tank when we left the show in the evening at about 8, then someone would have to come down at midnight to refill it, someone else at 4 a.m. and then we had to be there before 8 a.m. anyway, when the show opened to the public. The night it was Geoff's turn to do the 4 a.m. refill, he slept through the alarm, and we arrived at 8 the next morning to find this big soggy plastic dome collapsed all over the plants!'

In 1971 Frank Ward had been approached by Anglia Television to audition for a new gardening show they were planning called *Garden Diary.* 'I was terrified, but motivated by greed, so I went and did it and I was absolutely terrible. They reassured me that I wasn't, but they also asked if I knew anyone who might be good. I suggested Geoff, and I wish now I'd staked a claim for 10 per cent of his future earnings!'

Geoff told Radio Leicester in 1995 that he had gone along for an audition with about eight other people, some of whom were quite well-known names, so the competition was very tough. 'But because my lady was looking down on me again, this is what happened. What I had to do was to interview the presenter of their *Farming Diary* programme – about garden gnomes, would you believe? – and when I got there I discovered his wife had given birth the night before to their first baby and he had spent the whole morning in the pub, so he was none too sober. I asked him one question, and he did the rest and he was terrific. I have to say it was probably the best interview I have ever done in my life. He was really funny, really good, really incisive. At the end of it, the director said, "You didn't ask him many questions, did you?" and I said, "In my view the best interview is one where all you hear is the interviewee and the interviewer keeps quiet, because that's what people want to hear." He said, "You've got the job."'

Nick remembers it slightly differently. 'When he came to pick us up one Sunday he told us he'd been for the audition, but he didn't think he'd got it because everyone else had been in there for about half an hour and he'd been in for only five minutes, and they hadn't seemed particularly impressed with him. The following Sunday, when he came to pick us up, he told us he'd got the job.'

Whoever's version is correct, the director who auditioned him, Ron Downing, felt that Geoff was outstanding right from the start. 'He just took to it all, filming especially, so easily, and he came across as relaxed and natural, and seemed to understand the process of filming instinctively.'

The programmes, presented by Geoff and the nurseryman Adrian Bloom, were studio-based but included filmed inserts mainly of a practical nature 'We decided to do some items on building a rockery,' says Ron Downing, 'and were looking for somewhere to film it. In the end I suggested my own garden since I had plenty of room. We started in February to get ahead for the spring, but after the first day's filming, when we had got about half the rocks in, it snowed heavily overnight. For continuity, the next day we had to hose all the snow off, which turned the rockery into a mud bath, and we were packing it with peat to try to make it look like soil. But the rockery is still there – the small conifers Geoff planted have grown into big conifers now, and I have a constant reminder of Geoff every time I look out of my windows.'

Another permanent legacy of Geoff is Ron's York-stone paving. 'He rang me one day and said he'd just come back from Bradford, where they were taking up all the York paving and selling it for £10 a ton, so did I want some? I did indeed, and it was delivered one day when I was out. My wife and daughter had to unload it into huge piles. I never heard the end of that.'

The night the first programme was transmitted, Chris remembers being got out of bed with his brothers to watch Geoff on television. 'His first words were pure David Frost – "Hello, good evening and welcome!" – and then he said, "You don't have to have green fingers to be a good gardener." It was all very exciting the first time, I must say, and it was pretty exciting the second time. But by the fourth time, I really couldn't be bothered to get out of bed to go down and watch. It was only gardening, after all, and gardening was boring.'

On one memorable occasion Geoff was demonstrating how to prune a blackcurrant bush. He indicated the right point at which to make a cut, stressing the importance of using a good sharp knife. When he opened his own smart bone-handled pruning knife and started to cut, the blade was blunt. It transpired that someone had removed it from his pocket before they started filming and had blunted it as a joke.

Certainly, the fact that Geoff was on television didn't change the boys' lives. For one thing the programme was shown very late, so none of their friends were likely to see it, even by accident, and for another gardening didn't have the following it does now. 'And we would never have dreamt of going round saying, "Guess who my dad is!" ' says Nick. 'We're not like that and he wasn't like that either. He was always very modest about everything.'

The series was deemed a success and ran for over two years, but fell victim to the three-day week in 1973 when all television programmes ended at 10 p.m. So Geoff carried on with his print journalism and, in 1976, when the editorship of *Garden News*'s sister publication, the monthly *Practical Gardening*, fell vacant, Geoff applied for it. Much to Geoff Amos's surprise, he got it. 'I must say I didn't think he'd get it because he hadn't had all that much editorial experience, but he did, and he did a very good job.' He also carried on writing a column for *Garden News* which he did for the next 10 years.

Adrienne Wilde is now editor-in-chief of *Garden Answers* (into which *Practical Gardening* was absorbed in 1997) and *Garden News* as well as being the *Sunday Mirror*'s gardening columnist. She remembers that, at that time, the magazine was looking for a face-lift and

Geoff decided to make it a very down-to-earth magazine and, living up to its title, full of practical get-your-hands-dirty gardening. 'It was the time when *The Good Life* was very popular on television. Geoff was very keen on self-sufficiency and passionate about growing your own fruit and vegetables. So we did masses of step-by-step shots and features, not only about cultivation but also on how to bottle fruit and salt runner beans.'

Geoff took Adrienne on as technical writer on *Practical Gardening* in 1979. 'It was a very bizarre job interview, I must say, because Geoff then invited my husband at that time to come and see him, and asked him whether I could take the job! Like most men at that time, I suppose Geoff did have rather a sexist streak. He would say to me in those early days, "Oh, you like houseplants, don't you, and greenhouses," because they were considered soft, "women's" subjects, and the thought that I might be interested in growing vegetables never entered his head.'

In her first week she learnt a valuable lesson in time-management – the management of Geoff's time, that is. 'He gave me five features to write in that first week, and I realized afterwards that that was virtually a whole month's work for me. By getting me to do it all early on in the schedule, it meant he didn't wind up with a great pile of work to do at the end of it. He didn't mollycoddle you, either. He wasn't particularly lavish with praise, but he would reward effort and enthusiasm by giving you really interesting and challenging things to do.'

He also gave her a key piece of advice, which he followed himself throughout his career in journalism and broadcasting – remember who your readers are. 'Our readers don't have loads of money in their pockets,' he would say, 'but they have their passions and do want to have a go but are a bit nervous, so we must help them along, explain everything in straightforward language and be enthusiastic.'

'"Cheap and cheerful" was Geoff's mantra, and in every issue there would be some ideas you could knock up for "a couple of bob".

I remember when the orange box propagator made its first appearance in the magazine. Cyril (Geoff's father) actually made it for us, but whether it was Geoff's idea or Cyril's I don't know.'

After he and Colette separated, Geoff lived for a short while in a rented cottage near Peterborough, which had no land, just a concrete yard at the back. As he told Radio Leicester, 'For the first time in my life I woke up on a Saturday morning, saying, "What am I going to do with my weekend?" I'm a very active bloke, and I just couldn't take it. I came over to see my brother Tony, who lived at Langham, not far from Barnsdale, and he asked how I was doing. I said, "I think I'm going slowly mad, because I haven't got a bit of land to grow things on, and I've got to find some somewhere."'

As it happened, Tony knew someone near Oakham who had a couple of acres of land to rent, and though the cottage that went with it was occupied at the time, there was accommodation to be had in the stable block on the same estate, and Geoff took it on. It was part of the Barnsdale Hall Estate, now the Barnsdale Country Club.

'It was a lovely place because it was near Rutland Water,' Chris recalls. 'I remember seeing foxes playing out in the garden in the early morning. There were always interesting people visiting or working there, and I know he had a high old time. But it was grim. It was practically falling down, and it was cold and damp and squalid.' As Tony says, it was the sort of house where you wiped your feet on the way out. Once someone saw something scuttling across the floor and said, 'What's that?' and Geoff said, 'That? Oh, that's just my mouse.' An owl was nesting in the bathroom, but that wasn't a problem since Geoff didn't use it – half the ceiling had fallen into the bath. He did mention it to his landlord, Jim Dickenson. 'You might have cleaned the bath after you, Jim!'

Although his new accommodation was far from palatial, Geoff often had the boys to visit throughout this time and was very much a force in their teenage years. When Stephen was about 14, he decided he wanted to have his ear pierced and wear an earring. 'The first botched attempt was horrible. I got a mate to do it with a needle, and there was blood everywhere. Then I managed to get it done properly, but my mother was very upset about the fact that I was wearing an earring. So when the old man picked me up the following weekend, I got one of his talks. "How many doctors or lawyers do you ever come across wearing earrings? You'll never make a success of yourself with an earring. Rightly or wrongly people will look at that earring and say, 'I don't want to have you as my doctor or lawyer'." It all came flooding back years later when my elder daughter was born and the doctor had a whacking great earring and long hair! At the time I had no interest at all in becoming a doctor, and though I was thinking vaguely I might quite like to be a lawyer, this argument wasn't cutting much ice with me. In the end, after a lot more along these lines, he said, "More to the point, if you don't take it out, I'll take it out for you!" So I thought, all right. Seems fair enough. In that case I'll take it out. And in addition he bribed me. "I'll buy you a new set of bass guitar strings if you do." So that was a deal.'

Stephen by this time was passionate about music, but of course not the sort of music about which Geoff was passionate. When Stephen was 17, Geoff offered to give him driving lessons, but when he said he would rather have a new guitar instead, Geoff went along with it. He believed that the most important thing with kids is to create the opportunities for them to do what they want to do, and he stuck by that. Even though he would much rather Stephen had had the driving lessons, he let him have the guitar because that's what he really wanted to do. 'He did come and hear my band play once. I think he was probably appalled by it, but all he said afterwards was, "Why do you have to have it so loud? You really can't hear any of the words or the music," and "I don't understand why there has to be so much swearing in it." But I think he was probably quite proud that in the end we did actually get something recorded.'

Stephen admits that he was a bit of a problem for both his parents in his teenage years. He went to college, in theory to study law, economics, sociology and politics at A-level, but he wasn't interested in any of them, and even a change to arts subjects didn't help. In the end everyone concerned thought it would be better if he left. 'All I wanted to do was play music, and the old man used to say, "Well, that's fine as another string to your bow, but you really should work hard at school. If you do and you get your exams, you'll have a choice of any career you want. If you don't, you'll end up sweeping the streets and it'll be your mates you see driving by in a big Rolls-Royce with a lovely girl at their side. But if you do work hard and get your exams, you'll be the bloke in the Rolls!"'

That certainly wasn't the approach Geoff took with all his sons. It seems he tailored his advice to suit the boy, and whereas he thought that Stephen was too wild, too unconventional, and needed a little stability in his life, it seems as though he thought Chris needed a little more wildness. 'Once when I was staying with him, I was going to a party locally with my cousin Matt. He said, "What time do you want me to pick you up?" So I said, "About 11?" He said, "11?", so I said "All right, what about half-10, then?" He said "Half-10? What about 1 o'clock?"

'We used to have long discussions about the world when I was 15 or 16. He'd say, "We bring our kids up to want to have 2.4 children and a semi-detached house in Chingford because we think that's how they'll be happy. Why? They might be happier travelling the world and living in a tent"'.

Nick in a sense was the easiest of the three because he knew from quite early on that he wanted to go into horticulture too. 'When the old man started the garden centre, I used to spend a lot of time up there helping him. I don't know whether it started because it was a good way of spending time with Dad, but it suddenly grabbed hold and I soon became interested in all aspects of growing plants. He never pushed it on to any of us. It was a case of "Whatever you want to do, that's fine". I think memories of Rosie trying to push him and Tony into respectable careers made him very mindful of not pushing us into anything we didn't want to do 100 per cent. When I decided to go to horticultural college, though, he was delighted. He didn't force me to go to Writtle. He just didn't give me any other option! I went with him to the British Growers Look Forward exhibition at Harrogate when I was about 16, and he said, "Let's have a look at the Writtle stand," and that was the only stand we looked at.'

When Geoff took over the editorship of *Practical Gardening*, he decided that he would use some of his 2 acres to run trials for the magazine, but since the land was pretty overgrown he needed help to get it sorted out. As ever, Tony was roped in to give him a hand, and they found another willing volunteer, Carol Woods (now Carol Hamilton, and married to Tony). 'I worked for Ruddles Brewery as the receptionist, and in those days they had one sole surviving pub, the Noel Arms in Langham, which was in the same village as the brewery. So I'd finish work at 5 and then, when I didn't have anything else to do, I'd go and work behind the bar. Tony lived in Langham then and he used to come into the pub. Then he introduced me to Geoff. Those two were great fun when they got together. I'd always liked gardening, though I didn't know much about it then, and so I volunteered to go over there at weekends and help out in the garden.'

Cyril also used to spend time with Geoff at Barnsdale, helping him with various projects, especially those involving carpentry. He built the chicken coops when Geoff, in his self-sufficiency days, decided that keeping chickens would be a good thing.

In one of his rare flashes of business acumen, Geoff sometimes used to take photographs of himself in action, using a camera with a timer, and then sell them back to *Practical Gardening*. Since *Practical Gardening*, like all magazines, had quite long lead times, it sometimes meant that photographs for summer features had to be taken in spring, and so inevitably a little cheating went on. Adrienne Wilde recalls the time, early one spring, when they had to photograph Geoff harvesting lettuces. There was snow on the ground, which had to be carefully and thoroughly scraped off the soil, and some lettuces, purchased that morning at the local supermarket, were laid in neat rows on top of it. Nick, who witnessed all this going on, was horrified. 'You can't do that!' he told Geoff. 'Yes, I bloody well can,' he replied. 'But what if people find out?' Nick said. 'Well,' said Geoff, 'you're not going to tell them, and I'm certainly not going to tell them, so how are they going to find out?' (In fact, some readers did find out because, although they were diligent about scraping the snow from the deep-bed on which the lettuces were laid, they forgot about the snow in the fields at the back. Some sharp-eyed readers picked this up and there were a few embarrassing letters for Geoff to answer.)

Geoff worked very hard on the magazine, though his hours didn't always tally with everyone else's, as Adrienne Wilde recalls with admiration. 'Sometimes he would be out of the office most of the week, but he would come in on Friday afternoon at about 5, and he'd have written five good features by midnight. He was one of the few people I've ever come across who could burn the candle at both ends without the quality of the work suffering at all.'

He was also a good editor with an eye for talent. Alan Titchmarsh recalls meeting Geoff in the late 1970s when he was assistant editor on a rival publication, *Amateur Gardening*. Alan was strapped for cash, so Geoff suggested he might like to write a column for *Practical Gardening*. Alan was aghast at the thought. 'I can't do that,' he said, 'I'm under contract to *Amateur Gardening*.' 'Never mind that,' said Geoff. 'Do it under an assumed name.' So Alan became Tom Derwent, who wrote a regular column, and doing so solved his financial problem. As he later explained, 'I did it for security reasons – Social Security reasons.' Geoff once frightened the life out of Alan's wife Alison by ringing and asking for Mr Derwent, while pretending to be from the Inland Revenue.

In 1979 the cottage on the Barnsdale estate – Top Cottage – which went with the land Geoff had been gardening, became available to rent, so he moved out of the stable block and into the cottage. Although he had been cultivating part of the land for his *Practical Gardening* trials, the area closest to the cottage had been neglected for many years and was covered in brambles and nettles. Geoff didn't get round to sorting it out right away, which as things turned out worked to his advantage.

In those days, the BBC2 gardening programme *Gardeners' World*, made by BBC Midlands, was presented one week by Arthur Billitt from his own garden, Clack's Farm in Worcestershire, along with other presenters, including Peter Seabrook, Clay Jones and Geoffrey Smith, and for the following week's programme they would visit a large garden somewhere in the British Isles. They had to be large gardens then, because it wasn't possible to film in small gardens with huge Outside Broadcast vans, enormous cameras and the team of around 20 people needed to make the programme.

In 1979 the man who had been producing the BBC's farming programme for some years, John Kenyon, was made producer of *Gardeners' World*. Although in many respects Clack's Farm was a good location at which to base a gardening programme, because it was so large, John felt that it was perhaps a little too large and a little too perfect for most viewers to relate to.

'The night before we recorded a programme, I would wander round the garden with Arthur and, not being a gardener myself, I would ask, "Why is that plant not doing very well?" I wanted to know, and I felt that the viewers would, too, so I'd say, "Let's do something about it in the programme tomorrow." But when tomorrow came, the sick plant had gone and something healthy would be in its place because, as I learnt, Arthur never had failures! I was also aware that Arthur, lively and skilled as he was, was getting older and so couldn't go on for ever, and when he stopped, the programme would lose its base. So I was on the lookout for a new garden in which we could base the progamme, and word of it got out through a garden writer I knew, the late Graham Rose.

'One of the people who came to see me, funnily enough, was Alan Titchmarsh and, though I thought he would be very good, his garden was in the Home Counties, which was too far from our base in Birmingham, and it also meant that his garden would be three weeks ahead of most of the country. Then, one day, in Graham's kitchen, I met Geoff Hamilton. He was full of bullshit and told me all about the garden he was developing. Nevertheless, we got on very well because neither of us thought that gardening ought to be posh, and we weren't interested in presenting colour-supplement gardening.'

The upshot was that John Kenyon was persuaded to go and have a look at Barnsdale, as Top Cottage became known, to see whether they might be able to do one programme from there. 'It was an acre full of weeds and rubbish, basically,' John Kenyon says now. 'He had conned me!'

Geoff's version of the story is slightly different. 'He came up and he said, "Yes, I think we could make a programme from here," and then we walked into my little cottage, and outside the back it was head-high in brambles and weeds and goodness knows what. And he said, "What are you going to do with that?" and I said, "Well, I'm going to make a garden of it," and he said, "That would make a good series." And I was in.'

In those days television cameras were enormous heavy contraptions on wheels – four strong men were needed to lift them, and they had to have proper paths to move along, something that Barnsdale didn't have. So Tony and Carol were roped in to lay paving slabs ready for the cameras and also to put up a couple of greenhouses because the show had to go on even if the weather outside was appalling.

Geoff also realized that the garden wasn't up to scratch, so he went to recruit more help from his usual source – a pub, in this instance the Noel Arms in Whitwell, close to Barnsdale and to Rutland Water. 'I met Geoff orginally at the Fox and Hounds in Exton, another local village,' said Rod Biggs, 'but drinking had moved to the Noel Arms. We were both leaning against the bar one night, and Geoff asked me if I'd like a couple of days' casual work. Although I had worked as a school groundsman, I had no gardening experience, but Geoff was always good fun, so I took it.'

Clay Jones was the main presenter of that first programme from Barnsdale because he was experienced and was also a name, which Geoff then wasn't. But what John Kenyon liked about Geoff was his very different approach – the fact that he wore old jeans, an open-necked shirt and no tie was pretty revolutionary then, and his far from neat and tidy garden made a stark contrast with Clack's Farm. John realized quickly that Geoff also had the depth of knowledge that a presenter had to have if he were to be convincing. So while Clack's Farm continued as the show's main base, with Peter Seabrook and Arthur Billitt, there were more programmes from Barnsdale with Clay Jones or Geoffrey Smith as the main presenter. For some while, early on, Geoff was given a contract for only one programme at a time and was paid the princely sum of £50 a show.

While his television career was getting off the ground slowly, Geoff carried on as editor of *Practical Gardening* and, it must be said, he continued to play as hard as he worked. Fay Howison, whose husband Dan was Head of Modern Languages at Oakham School, the public school in the town, recalls meeting Geoff in Exton at a party in the late 1970s. 'The room was quite crowded and the lights were low, and I was dancing with Dan. He suddenly started to get a bit wild, whirled me round so that I shut my eyes, and when I opened them I was dancing with someone completely different whom I had never seen in my life before – Geoff Hamilton. He was very merry and told me all about being a journalist, which I found very interesting and we chatted away for a long time. The next time we met, he had absolutely no recollection of that meeting at all!'

Even so, the Howisons, Geoff, Tony and his first wife, and Carol, all became very good friends, and one night during a power cut in Rutland Fay rang them all up to say that since they had a piano with candlestick holders on it, why didn't everyone go there for a singsong round the piano in the dark. 'We all had such a thoroughly good time,' Tony recalls, 'that we started to meet every Sunday evening in one of the group's homes, and so the Exton Singers was formed. We'd have a jolly good sing and then wind up at the Noel Arms in Whitwell, which became our pub.' Geoff was a bass and Tony a tenor, not because their voices were very different, Tony says, but only because Geoff got there five minutes earlier than he did and took the last bass position. They sang carols at Christmas, madrigals, sacred music, folk-songs, and Geoff, Tony, Dan and another friend, Alan McComie Smith, even formed a barbershop quartet from within the group. Geoff and Tony did some good old cockney songs – grandfather Alf's influence, perhaps – like 'Any Old Iron' and 'What a Mouth' as well as a fine rendition of 'Underneath the Arches', Flanagan and Allen's greatest hit, complete with moth-eaten fur coat and a hat with the brim pushed up at the front. They did concerts for charity, singing at old people's homes and in pubs – 'We were the only singing group I know that was once offered a pound to leave a pub!'

They also did themed evenings sometimes. Once, they were invited to take part in a Victorian evening and, having thought about what the Victorians were most interested in, decided to take death as their theme. So they sang 'The Lost Chord', 'The Long Day Closes', 'Old Abraham Brown is Dead and Gone' and 'Old Black Joe' and performed two readings to a softly hummed version of Chopin's funeral march. The first was a solemn intonation of all the different expressions for dying – to pop one's clogs, to drop off the edge of the plate, to shuffle off one's mortal coil – and the second was the reading of a bankrupt Victorian undertaker's inventory: 'coffins, pine – ten; coffins, oak – two; gravel, green – one ton…'

Geoff also found the group shared his love of word games, and there were crazes for anagrams. Fay, for example, was Showy Fiona, Dan was something quite unprintable, involving an unspeakable act in a wardrobe, and Tony became Nathan Y. Monolith. Shortly after being ceremonially annointed with his anagram, Tony began to receive catalogues for thermal underwear through the post addressed to 'Mr N.Y. Monolith'. Of course, he knew who was responsible, but it was never admitted. Geoff stayed as Thin Loam until he moved up in the world in the 1980s, when he was given the much more appropriate handle of General Sir Toffo hyphen Times.

Limericks were also a great source of delight, often done as joint ventures on the phone and involving so much helpless laughter that it would take minutes to get even a couple of words out. Fay remembers the occasion when Geoff, as a gardening writer, was invited to enter a competition to compose a Christmas limerick for a new sort of garden hose called Lifecell.

'There were good prizes on offer, like a crate of champagne, so we worked quite hard at it and came up with a number of entries, some of which we wouldn't have dared send in. The one that sticks in my mind was, "When Santa hoves in from infinity/With Lifecell for all the vicinity/The Christmas tree fairy/Had better be wary/If she wants to retain her virginity." The last line was definitely Geoff's. It was disqualified on the grounds of obscenity, so you can imagine what some of those we didn't dare enter were like, but we did win a crate of champagne with one of the others.'

Mock obituaries also became popular for a while, and Fay recalls a party to which someone had brought some party poppers. They were such a novelty then that Fay didn't know what they were and

Geoff and his father Cyril in the greenhouse at New Road, Broxbourne, with their much-loved chrysanthemums.

Happy holidays: Geoff and Colette on the beach at Woolacombe with the boys (*top left and right, and above*); Nick's fifth birthday with (left to right) Chris, Nick and Stephen (*right*).

Geoff 'the nurseryman' during his college days.

Geoff minding the shop – Hamilton's Garden Centre in Kettering in the early 1970s.

The staff at the first Barnsdale – Carol Woods (now Hamilton),
Geoff and Rod Biggs.

Staff at the second Barnsdale – Carol,
Ian Spence and Lorraine Shone.

Sue Darlington, Geoff's secretary
for 12 years, now married to Nick.

Early days of *Gardeners' World* at the first Barnsdale, with Geoffrey Smith (left),
Clay Jones (right) and the bulky, heavy outside broadcast equipment needed then.
Carol Hamilton and Fay Howison look on.

The first Barnsdale.

Above left:Virgin territory – the second Barnsdale, 1984.

Above centre, above right, and left: The evolution of the former vegetable garden at the new Barnsdale – first cottage garden, then Mediterranean garden.

An area of the courtyard in 1984 (*left*) and in 1992 (*right*).

'Ullo, saileur! Geoff the matelot, with Carol (right) and Nancy as French tarts.

The Exton Singers in medieval garb. Geoff is in the centre at the back and Lynda on the far left.

Geoff in 'Versailles' at the new Barnsdale. He had the choice between buying a new suit
or this splendid urn as a focal point. No contest.

inadvertently fired one, hitting her husband Dan in the eye. 'He was hurt, so he retired upstairs to bathe the eye and decided he wouldn't come down again. So Geoff wrote him an obituary, "Here lie the bones of one-eyed Dan/A very much abusèd man/His wife, after only one small highball/Shot the poor bugger in the eyeball." When I went upstairs and repeated this to Dan, he roared with laughter and decided he would come back down and join the party after all.'

If there was a group headquarters, it was the Noel Arms in the tiny village of Whitwell, population about 77, whose landlord Sam Healy and his family shared a similar sense of humour. Both Geoff and Tony had a habit of leaning one forearm on the bar, facing each other. One day Sam's son came in with a pile of books and simply placed them on the bar between the two human bookends.

The Noel Arms was also the scene for one of the best japes they ever played, the twinning of Whitwell with Paris. The gang had been in the bar at the Noel bemoaning the fact that Rutland was losing its identity. This was long before the decision to do away with Rutland altogether and merge it into Leicestershire – a decision that Geoff never accepted; he remained living in Rutland all his life. (The country was reinstated subsequently.) It was more to do with the fact that Rutland Water was a mecca for fishermen from all over the north, so the voices heard in the pub were more Barnsley than Barnsdale. 'We began to think of ways in which we could put Whitwell on the map,' Tony recalls. 'Someone suggested that what other villages did was twin themselves with a village on the Continent. This seemed like a good idea until someone else pointed out that what was likely to happen was that Whitwell would be twinned with a tiny village on the Continent that no one had ever heard of, and what would be the point of that? Then someone said, "Why not twin Whitwell with Paris?" Well, that was it.'

Everyone warmed to the idea. They got a letterhead printed with 'Jumelage de Whitwell sur Mer' on it – they weren't 'sur mer'; they were 'sur reservoir' but no one knew the French for 'reservoir'! – and a letter was duly written to Jacques Chirac, then mayor of Paris, pointing out the many similarities between Paris and Whitwell. Paris had the River Seine; Whitwell had Rutland Water. Paris had the Moulin Rouge; Whitwell had the Noel Arms, and so on. Therefore, twinning the two was clearly a good idea. The letter ended, 'Would this be all right?' – a phrase that seemed so typically English it was bound to carry weight in diplomatic circles.

Not surprisingly, perhaps, they didn't get a reply initially so, thinking they wouldn't get one at all, they decided to go ahead anyway and have a twinning day celebration, with everyone dressed up in French clothes. Sam Healy said that if they thought they could get 60 people to come to the Noel Arms, he would have a marquee put up in the car park.

In the event over 700 people turned up, all in costume. There were lots of French tarts and onion sellers. Geoff was a matelot, Cyril came as a very stylish gigolo and Rosie as an equally stylish madame, while Tony was a gendarme, in hired uniform, directing the traffic with his baton and whistle. 'I stopped a car and told the woman driver, "Ze piss-urp is in ze purb." A very bemused lady looked me straight in the eye and said, "I'm off to a piss-up of my own in Stamford, thank you very much," and drove on.' There was a band consisting of a trumpet, drums, a banjo and a violin – as Tony says, when there's a population of only 77 you have to take what you can get. There was also a Jacques Chirac lookalike standing on the passenger seat of a Renault, with his head sticking out through the sunroof, acknowledging the cheers of the crowd.

A brigadier came in full uniform, complete with a corporal as his driver and a little official-looking flag on the bonnet of the car. 'He was trying to get into the marquee but was refusing to have his wrist stamped by the man dressed as the Pope on the door. He kept saying, "I will not have my wrist stamped. Why can't you stamp my driver twice?" We were very impressed with the act, but then it turned out he was a real brigadier who just happened to be passing through the area.'

The highlights of the day's events were the dedication of the pissoir in the pub yard and the unveiling of the specially made signs saying 'Twinned with Paris' which had been welded to the two road signs at either end of the village.

Astonishingly, a few weeks after the event they received a reply from Jacques Chirac, thanking them for their letter and saying he was rather embarrassed to tell them that Paris was already twinned – with Rome. But the deed was done. A newspaper covering the event went to the trouble of checking the international regulations concerning twinning and discovered that you didn't need the permission of the place with which you wanted to twin before you went ahead. The rules have been changed subsequently, whether as a direct result of Whitwell's twinning with Paris no one knows, but the position stands and Whitwell is officially twinned with Paris, so as you drive through the village on the main road between Oakham and Stamford, 'Twinned with Paris' signs are still there today.

The day after the celebrations, Geoff had to travel to Heathrow to meet a party of *Practical Gardening* readers with whom he was flying to Vancouver on a holiday organized by the magazine. Having got himself together in a bit of a rush, he had forgotten to wash off the fake moustache he had pencilled on the day before, so he received a bunch of bemused travellers looking like a worn-out version of Inspector Clouseau.

The following November, Dan and Fay invited a colleague of Dan's at Oakham School to join the Exton Singers, then starting rehearsals for their Christmas carol singing, in aid of Save the Whale. Lynda Irving, now Lynda Hamilton, taught French and Latin. Having recently been divorced, she had moved to Oakham with her two sons, Jeremy and William, then ten and seven, at the start of the autumn term. 'We both liked her very much,' Fay Howison recalls. 'She'd had a pretty tough time when her marriage broke up, and she had the most beautiful soprano voice. So we threw a little party for her to meet the rest of the gang.'

Lynda's first impression of Geoff, and indeed her abiding memory, is of his laughter, of a man with a big personality, a great sense of fun and the ability to turn anything into a joke. Although her father had been a great Percy Thrower fan and watched *Gardeners' World* regularly, she had no idea who Geoff was until, at their second singing rehearsal, someone pointed him out as 'our local celebrity'.

Later, Geoff told her he saw her as a challenge, thinking that her background was more sophisticated and up-market than it actually was. 'Geoff used to say what attracted him to me was my Jaeger coat. It wasn't Jaeger at all – it was John Lewis, which just about sums it all up, really. We hit it off immediately and went out together a few times, but neither of us wanted commitment then.' So over the next few years they saw each other regularly through the singing and at parties, but not until 1985 did they decide they really wanted to be together.

Meanwhile, Geoff's career was beginning to take off. He wrote his first four books in 1980 – most appropriately in a series published by David & Charles called 'Penny Pinchers'. They were *Growing Soft Fruits, Herbs and How to Grow Them, Design and Build a Patio or Terrace* and *Design and Build a Rockery*. They were more booklets than books, full of practical advice and line drawings, and they sold moderately well. Geoff's television career was also beginning to gather speed. By the end of 1981 Barnsdale became the programme's main base, and, since Geoffrey Smith decided he didn't want to do the programme any longer, Geoff became a regular presenter, along with Clay Jones.

John Kenyon and Geoff got on extremely well because they both had the same idea of who the programme was for. 'We always aimed to appeal to the ordinary gardener. My thesis was that there were a hell of a lot of people out there with gardens, and they did want advice about what to do and when. That became the philosophy of the whole programme. I don't really think *Gardeners' World* had had a philosophy before that. I felt it had lacked editorial direction, and I felt it ought to reflect practical ideas and muddy boots.'

Obviously, when Geoff started out as a presenter, he was inexperienced and nervous, but he was given very good advice that he followed to great effect. John Kenyon told him very early on that the only way to get away with anything is by being yourself. If you are going to be the straightforward down-to-earth gardener, then it's quite idiotic to be clever clever. Clay Jones added his own succinct pearl of wisdom: 'Never lie to the viewers. Remember they can see the whites of your eyes!'

Whereas previous gardening presenters like Percy Thrower and Arthur Billitt had always been experts, handing down information to the viewers, Geoff came across as a gardener like the rest of us, keen to share his ideas and knowledge. One of John Kenyon's reasons for moving on from Clack's Farm was that nothing ever appeared to go wrong there and no mistakes were ever made, so he was very keen for Geoff to show that he did get it wrong sometimes, and not everything worked.

'In one trial,' John Kenyon recalls, 'Geoff sowed sweetcorn under a sheet of black polythene. Part of the experiment was to exclude all light until the seeds had germinated, so we couldn't take a peek and check on progress. When we got Clay and Geoff to pull the polythene sheeting off on camera, the bed was full of the weed fat-hen and you couldn't see any sweetcorn at all! He took some persuading initially to let the viewers see things like that, but to his credit he quickly realized that showing things that hadn't worked and owning up to mistakes added enormously to his reputation and popularity. Things went wrong for the viewers in their gardens, and so they identified very strongly with Geoff when things went wrong in his.

It also added greatly to his credibility, because if he was honest about things that didn't work, then viewers believed him when he told them about things that did.'

It was almost inevitable that, once he began to relax in front of a camera, someone as full of humour as Geoff would want to have a laugh with the viewers as well. On one occasion in the *£2 a Week Garden* he used tinfoil trays from a Chinese take-away for sowing seedlings and was showing on camera how to prick them out. 'The trouble with pricking out lettuces from Chinese take-away trays,' he said, 'is that an hour later you feel like pricking out another one.' John Kenyon let him get away with that one, but when Geoff attempted another joke he came down hard. 'I told him to leave the jokes to Morecambe and Wise, because I do think it is the hardest thing in the world to be really funny on television. The only thing you can be, I believe, is yourself. Yes, Geoff did have a great sense of humour, but what people liked most about him was his friendliness and helpfulness.'

It was advice that Geoff took to heart. When I started working with him in the late 1980s, he would be very funny while we were getting ready to do something, but the jokes disappeared once the camera was running. When I knew him better and asked him why he wouldn't show that side of himself, he repeated what John Kenyon had told him.

With the BBC turning up to film at the garden every couple of weeks – and they were whole programmes then, not just segments in the magazine format that *Gardeners' World* adopted later – Geoff realized that he needed more help to get ready for the programme. So Rod Biggs, who had gone to Barnsdale originally for a couple of days' casual labour, became a permanent member of staff, and so did Carol Woods, who gave up her job at the brewery and behind the bar of the Noel Arms at Langham. 'I had never previously even thought about taking up gardening as a job, but then the opportunity had presented itself, and I loved it, and found I had an aptitude for it. Geoff taught me a great deal and, generous man that he was, he then paid for me to go to college one day a week to do my City & Guilds in horticulture, which took me three years. I got a distinction in the final exam, and I was named student of the year. Geoff was as excited as I was and even came with me to the presentation. Not many bosses would do that.'

Rod remembers those early days as being enormous fun. Before each visit Geoff would decide what was likely to be wanted for the programme, and they would get it ready. 'But then the BBC would arrive, and they'd decide to do something quite different and it would be, "Rod, can you get that ready?"' The occasional bit of cheating for the cameras did go on, but only when strictly necessary. At one stage, for reasons of economy, they would film two programmes at a time – one to go out that Friday and the other to go out two weeks later. 'One year we had some very late snow in spring, which wasn't a problem at all for the programme going out that week because everyone else had had some snow that week. But it was extremely unlikely that there'd be snow around two weeks later, so I had to clear all the snow from the main garden, the lawn, the beds and so on. It took me a good hour of hard shovelling and then spraying off the last bit. I didn't always watch the programmes go out, I must admit, but I did watch that one, and if you looked carefully, you could see snow on the ground just beyond the greenhouses and, had the camera panned round another foot or two, you would have seen the 6-foot snowpile that I'd cleared!'

Something rather similar went on for the cover photograph of the first book Geoff wrote for the BBC in 1981, the *Gardeners' World Vegetable Book*. There's Geoff bent over his hoe in the veg plot, with snow clearly visible on the grass beyond the fence, and a most interesting assortment of vegetables growing together – white cabbage, summer lettuce, new potatoes, maincrop carrots and aubergines – the best, in fact, that the local greengrocer could provide.

As well as help in the garden, Geoff – or rather Geoff's friends – realized that he needed help in the house as well. While the cottage at Barnsdale was in much better repair than the stables had been, he still treated it as just a place to rest his head and not even his worst enemy could have accused him of bring house-proud. Margaret Oliver was invited to go to see him. 'He asked me what my rate was per hour, and when I told him he said, "I'll pay you more than that!" He was still at *Practical Gardening* when I started, so he was never there when I came. He'd leave my money on the table, but it was always more than he owed me, so I always left him change until the day I found a stiff note saying the money he left was all for me, so would I please not bother giving him change! He was a typical bachelor in those days. I was always picking up money that had fallen out of his trouser pockets when he had simply dropped them on the bedroom floor the night before.'

The major source of grief for Mrs O, or Mrs O'Liver as Geoff always called her, was the state of the kitchen floor when the BBC came. The only loo was upstairs, so everyone had to trail through the kitchen in their muddy boots, leaving the York-stone floor looking more like a ploughed field. 'I did suggest to him one day that it might be easier all round if he sowed grass on it! He just laughed and left me to get on with cleaning it up!'

Everything was going well for Geoff until April 1981 when Cyril died suddenly of a heart attack. Mark was the one who dealt with it. 'Cyril died in the bathroom, with a smile on his face, a little Buddha smile. There was nothing horrific about it, and I wasn't at all shocked by his appearance after death. His eyes were half-open, and so I closed them and gave him a little kiss on his forehead. Neither Geoff nor Tony wanted to see him at the funeral home. They just couldn't face it.'

Geoff was absolutely devastated by Cy's death, as Chris, his youngest son, recalls. 'I was talking to him on the phone the day it had happened, but I didn't know. Afterwards, I thought he sounded odd and mentioned it to Nick, and Nick said, "I think he's worried about Grandpa." So I rang him back and he said, "Oh yes, Grandpa's gone to hospital, but he's not dead or anything." But he was dead. He just couldn't bring himself to tell us on the phone. He came round later to tell us face to face, and he was so upset. Although I was very close to my grandpa, I wanted to cry not because he was dead but because the old man was so upset.'

Although Tony adored his father too, he believes Geoff missed him more because, on top of everything else, they shared a love of gardening and Cyril had been his inspiration.

When I first worked with Geoff in February 1988, my only brother had been killed in a car crash about six weeks earlier. Geoff was very kind, and we'd sat in his car talking about what it meant to lose someone close. He said that after Cyril died, he had gone out into the garden, thrown himself down on the grass and howled with grief. And then, he said, he had got up, and got on with it. And that's precisely what Geoff did. He threw himself into his work.

Gardeners' World went from strength to strength, with Geoff developing new gardens for the programme. Of all those early garden projects, the one people remember most vividly is the £2 a *Week Garden*. From the beginning of his career as a journalist, Geoff had been very conscious that most gardeners don't have a fortune to spend on their gardens, hence all the cheap and cheerful projects for 'a couple of bob' that were a prominent feature of his tenure at *Practical Gardening*. So in January 1983 Geoff started planning his £2 a *Week Garden*. He put himself in the position of a young man with a wife and one small child who had just bought a house with a very small garden measuring 36 by 48 feet (11 by 14.5 m). What with finding the deposit, paying the mortgage, lashing out on carpets, curtains, paint and wallpaper, there would be very little left to spend on the garden. Geoff felt that £2 a week (about £5 in today's terms) would be reasonable, but that sum had to cover not only the development and maintainance of an attractive ornamental garden but would also have to keep the family of three in fruit and vegetables as well. Since Geoff had already created one garden from a completely bare site, and since it would have been stretching even his ingenuity to the limits to do it for a mere £2 a week, he made a few assumptions about what would already be there, like some basic tools – a spade, a fork, a rake and a couple of hoes, and a cheap lawn mower. There was a small area of paving, one tree (a crab apple), two shrubs (a kerria and a berberis) and a very small greenhouse. Geoff did ponder long and hard about the greenhouse, but felt in the end that it would increase the range of gardening activities and would allow him to save money by growing lots of plants from seed.

He thought that he might find it rather depressing, having to scrimp and save and improvise, but in the event the reverse was true. 'I enjoyed every minute of it,' he wrote in the introduction to the booklet that accompanied the series. 'Someone – and I just wish I could remember who – once wrote about the pleasure to be found in making small economies, and by George he was right. I well remember racking my brains for days to find a way of saving the £90 it would have cost me to buy a cloche to cover one of my vegetable beds. It's hard to believe but, like Archimedes, it came to me in the bath. In a flash of inspiration, I saved myself £85 at a stroke, and it was all I could do to stop myself leaping naked from the bath and running from the house shouting Eureka! It was only the prospect of a £90 fine that stopped me.'

The cause of the excitement was the home-made cloche made from alkathene water pipe, bamboo canes and polythene sheeting which made its first appearance on *Gardeners' World* in this garden, but by no means its last! The *£2 a Week Garden* was full of Geoff's money-saving ideas – a plastic dustbin bag used as a compost container, hanging baskets made of pieces of timber used for packing cases that he found in a factory, the cold frame made from an apple box, a sheet of plastic and a couple of onion sacks for shading, this last another idea that cropped up again and again over the years.

In the greenhouse, in addition to the famous Chinese take-away foil containers, the polystyrene trays on which meat, fish and fruit are sold in supermarkets were also used as seed trays, along with plastic coffee cups, cut-down cardboard milk cartons as pots for individual seeds and cuttings and papier-mâché egg boxes as modules for the multiple sowing of vegetable crops. He made his own grow bags and his own pots from thick plastic sacks, lashing out on one whale-hide pot from the garden centre to use as a pattern for the other 63 pots he needed, and using an ordinary office stapler to fix them together. Another invention that made its first appearance here was the Barnsdale windowsill propagator, a cut-down cardboard box lined with tinfoil to reflect light all round the seedlings and prevent them from growing in one direction and becoming weak and spindly.

As for the plants, there were lots of penny-pinching ideas too. He grew shrubs and climbers from cuttings and lots of different types of plants from seed – not just vegetables and annuals, but also alpines and some perennials. In many cases he raised more plants than he needed for his little garden to swap with other gardeners for plants he couldn't raise himself – another excellent way of saving money. The lawn, which was not in great shape, had to make do with regular mowing to encourage the grass and to weaken and then kill off many of the broad-leaved weeds, and a dose of Growmore in April and July. Coarse weeds like dandelions were treated with kitchen salt, and to treat moss, the result of poor drainage in one area, Geoff spiked over the area with a fork, then brushed in coarse grit to lighten the soil and improve the drainage.

By the end of the season, Geoff had got a number of valuable points across to his viewers. Perhaps the main one was that the one area of gardening you really can't afford to skimp on is preparing the soil. The more organic matter you can work in right at the start, the better the plants will grow, the more productive your garden will be and the better it will look.

Geoff took it very seriously – so much so that some viewers thought he must be on his uppers and sent him small donations – and he really didn't cheat. John Kenyon made sure of that. Every week he would march round the garden with Geoff and demand to know the provenance and the exact cost of anything new. Admittedly, rather than operate on £2 every week, he took a whole year's budget – £104 – and worked to that because obviously there are times in the year – spring in particular – when you need to spend a great deal more than you do in June or in December. As he wrote in the booklet, 'So if you're not to run into what my bank manager calls "cash flow" problems, you'll need to put something away in the cheaper months to allow yourself to splash out a bit in the spring. That's known as saving for a sunny day!'

Although he made a very careful record of how much he saved by checking at the greengrocer's the prices of the fruit and vegetables he harvested, he didn't plough it back into the garden. Instead, he saved it and by the end of the season it totalled £140. Since he had spent only £95 on the garden, that meant he'd made a profit of £43 – not enough to put him in the millionaire bracket, as he said, but at least enough to let him buy a proper watering can and return the teapot to the kitchen.

But although Geoff was pleased to have come out in the black, what gave him the most pleasure, of course, was the sense of achievement that he got from improvising and doing things himself – not a discovery in his case, but simply a reminder, because it was something he had been doing all his life. 'There's a local farmer round here,' Geoff wrote, 'who drives a white Mercedes and lives in a very grand house and who must be worth half a million if he's worth a penny. But he still repairs his own shoes. Of course the locals all laugh and put it down to meanness. But, curious, I asked him one day why he did it. He gave me two reasons. Firstly it served to remind him of the days when he didn't have what he has now, so that he never takes it for granted. But the main reason is the sense of satisfaction he gets from using his hands and from making a fine job of what he does. After the year of the £2 experiment, I know exactly what he means.'

While Geoff's love of improvising and making something out of nothing didn't always endear him to people in the horticultural trade, who would much rather we spent £90 on one of their cloches rather than knock one up ourselves, it was extremely important to him for just the same reasons as the farmer's. Even in later life, when he did splash out on something like a reproduction Victorian lantern cloche, you always got the feeling that this was going very slightly against the grain and that at the back of his mind he was probably thinking, 'Now with a few roofing laths and some clear polycarbon sheeting…'

By mid-1983 Geoff began to realize that 2 acres of land weren't really enough for his needs any longer. What's more, the land was only rented, so it didn't make sense to pour money into something he didn't own. He couldn't buy it, because the whole of the Barnsdale Hall Estate was about to be sold off and be turned into a country club. So he started looking round for somewhere bigger, somewhere to buy.

CHAPTER FIVE

THE BARNSDALE STORY

When Rod Biggs moved into the Oakham area, before he even met Geoff, he had stayed with a group of friends at The Grange, about a mile away from Barnsdale on the other side of the main Oakham to Stamford road. They were renting the house, a small Victorian stone farmhouse, from the owners, who decided in late 1983 that they wanted to sell it, along with 5 acres (2 hectares) of land. When Rod heard that the property was on the market he could hardly contain his excitement and knocked Geoff up one night to tell him about it. Geoff immediately saw the vision of a new, expanded Barnsdale, where he could do all the things he really wanted to do, but couldn't because of space restrictions at his current plot. So that night he went to reconnoitre and, since he was a man with his priorities straight, the main objective of his mission was to test the soil. Out came the soil auger, and before long he was loaded with little bags of soil, which he was to carry back to Top Cottage to test. But while he was there he just couldn't resist the opportunity to peer in through the windows and was quite taken aback when he saw the hippie décor, with psychedelic orange and purple swirly paintwork. Not exactly Victorian, he thought, but only in need of a pot or two of paint and a bit of elbow grease.

The soil was fine – more or less neutral, though it was heavy, full of stones and badly compacted. Geoff got very excited about The Grange. It was ideal for his purposes – plenty big enough for a good few years of television gardening programmes and, as it was surrounded by farmland, there was the possibility of acquiring a bit more land in the future. There was a fine solid stone barn and a range of other outbuildings, which could be used as stores and workshops, and, best of all for a man who loved his solitude, the property was hidden from the road by a line of large, mature trees. It was also very close to the existing Barnsdale, which would make the move relatively straightforward.

There was only one snag – The Grange was on the market at £100,000, and at that point Geoff had precisely £8 in the bank. But he was never one to let a good opportunity pass him by or a mere detail get in the way, so he set to work trying to raise the finance. He was lucky in that his bank manager turned out to be friendly, but even friendly bank managers need some reassurance that the loan will be safe.

'Geoff came to me one day,' John Kenyon recalls, 'and said, "Are you prepared to commit perjury on my behalf?" He explained the situation, so I wrote a letter to his bank manager on BBC notepaper saying that Geoff Hamilton was very much a part of the BBC's plans for the future of gardening on television, and that I could guarantee that his income would increase over the next few years. Of course, I couldn't actually guarantee any such thing, but I felt sure that what I was saying was true.'

Those three letters – BBC – worked their usual magic, and the bank manager agreed to lend the money, though Geoff still had to find a small deposit, and someone who would act as guarantor for the loan. Some good friends lent him the money for the deposit and Tony, ever ready to risk his all for his brother, agreed to act as guarantor. 'What the bank didn't know was that I hadn't got any money either, but it all worked out in the end, so they never needed to find out!'

The deal was done at the beginning of 1984, and Geoff moved in.

The BBC decided that it would be too confusing for viewers if The Grange kept its original name, so it became 'Barnsdale'. Geoff and Tony went to look at the land together. 'It was very heavy and covered in grass that was waist high. I said to Geoff, "What on earth are you going to do with it?" He just smiled and said, "Leave it to me."'

The first thing he did was to get a local farmer to plough the land with a mole plough, designed to tunnel into heavily compacted soil to aerate and drain it. But the soil was still very heavy and stony, and it took years of hard work and many tonnes of organic matter – most of it home-made compost – to get it to the workable state in which viewers saw it. Geoff would grit his teeth in future years when people said to him, 'Oh, it's all right for you! You've got lovely soil at Barnsdale.'

The next job was to lay on water and to put up a greenhouse, so that there would always be somewhere to film even when it was too wet to work outside or there was snow on the ground.

The site was very open – just a field, basically – and flat, and John Kenyon felt something had to be done very quickly. Geoff suggested that he put in a dozen good-sized trees right away. John agreed, so they set about this very daunting task and filmed the whole thing. They were big, mature trees, with huge root-balls, which had to be transported on giant articulated trucks and planted with a sizeable mobile crane. It made very dramatic television, and getting some height into the flat patch of land instantly made a big difference.

When Geoff moved into Barnsdale, the garden was just the area immediately around the house – the woodland areas in the front and to the side, and the walled garden to the rear of the house. Geoff walked round and round his new empire for a full three weeks before he decided what he wanted to do – by which time he had a clear and exciting vision in his mind. First, he would break through the wall and install a gate, to create a vista in what, at the time, was just a rough field. To Geoff, this would be the centrepiece for the whole site, the pivot around which the rest would be developed as and when the BBC needed to create new, small gardens for *Gardeners' World*.

So the starting-point was the area immediately outside the gate. John Kenyon told him what he needed was a decent pavilion and a croquet lawn, but Geoff settled for a wide sweep of lawn with a beech hedge at the far end to screen the rest of the undeveloped land, with a large urn as a focal-point in front of it and deep herbaceous borders on either side. Geoff was still strapped for cash, but he knew that the urn had to be something special. He was thinking about splashing out on a new suit to wear to press receptions, so now it was a toss-up between the suit and the urn. Given Geoff's attitude to clothes, there are no prizes for guessing which of the two he chose. Without the pavilion and croquet hoops, the area still had sufficient grandeur and style for John Kenyon to christen the area 'Versailles' – a name that has stuck until the present day.

Of course, when Geoff moved from Barnsdale 1 to Barnsdale 2, he was not so much moving house as moving garden, and move the garden he did, with the help of Carol, Rod and Betty Franklin, the part-time secretary he had then. 'The old garden was fairly well planted up then, even though the plants had only been there a year or two,' Carol recalls, 'so we dug up nearly every one that could be moved, potted them all up and moved them up the road to the new garden. We didn't have a van or anything – we just moved them in our cars, so you can imagine it took a long time, and each of us ended up with a car full of soil. The plants stood in serried ranks in the courtyard garden behind the house, where they had to be fed and watered, just like Geoff himself, because the land was nowhere near ready for planting then. And with no room in the greenhouse, anything slightly tender had to stand in the house in bad weather.'

The chickens were also moved from the old Barnsdale, and this time they had a mobile run that could be moved around the garden so that, in theory anyway, the chickens would eat the pests in one area before being moved on to the next. In practice, though, they were more trouble than they were worth. Geoff was far too sentimental to wring their necks once their laying days were over, so they just lived on, never laying a single egg, and died a natural death, on which they were all given a decent burial under the old apple tree. No military honours, but at least Geoff felt they had had a dignified send-off. 'The last survivor had the run of the place,' Carol remembers, 'and she used to go into the house through the cat flap and eat the dog's food. She also had a gammy leg and would strut round the yard doing the goose-step, like an SS officer.'

Moss, Geoff's black and white Border collie, came as a puppy soon after Geoff moved in, and being a very sociable dog was always around whenever the crew came to film. 'Geoff loved that dog,' Chris remembers. 'He was quite keen on the ladies, was Moss, and he used to go off, sometimes for a day or so if there was one in the village that he had his eye on. But I remember once he went missing for a couple of months. Geoff really thought he'd gone for good, and he was distraught. But, like a bad penny, he turned up again and there was a deliriously happy reunion. It was drinks all round that night. Moss died just two weeks after the old man. It's a good thing that he died first. The old man would have been heartbroken.' There is a theory that Moss gave up the ghost when his master died.

There was wildlife at Barnsdale, too, and while Geoff was always keen to encourage some of it into the garden, not all of God's creatures were equally welcome. Rabbits, for example, were a major problem. It was almost impossible to carry out vegetable trials because as soon as young plants were planted out, or seedlings appeared, the rabbits would demolish them. They experimented with an electric fence to keep them out, Rod Biggs recalls, with three wires, spaced at precise distances so that in theory the rabbits could not get through. 'They would either jump over the fence or crawl under it, and the only creatures that ever got a shock from it were Moss, a couple of toads and me. So we abandoned that and took on the gigantic task of fencing the entire site with chicken wire instead, buried deep enough to stop them burrowing under it.'

Rod's wife Amanda also worked at Barnsdale. They had met at the first Barnsdale where she was employed to do Geoff's books, but like all the office staff she had soon found herself roped in to help in the garden too. Early on, when hardly any of the garden at the new Barnsdale was developed, she used to keep her pony there, fenced in to keep it off the few areas that were cultivated. 'One day we spotted that the pony was out and heading for the vegetable trial beds,' Rod remembers. 'I quickly pulled some carrots to entice her away, but she wasn't having any and tried to bolt past me. I grabbed hold of her, but she kept on going, so there I was doing an inadvertent Cossack act, clinging on to the bridle for dear life. Eventually, I did manage to stop her, and a potential disaster was averted.'

Perhaps the most serious problem the *Gardeners' World* team faced at Barnsdale was the fact that only a mile or so away was the end of the runway at RAF Cottesmore – the NATO training base for Tornado pilots. There are dozens of examples recorded for posterity on videotape showing Geoff's piece to camera interrupted by the deafening scream of Tornadoes playing follow-my-leader over the garden at what seemed like 500 feet, to be greeted with his favourite expletive, 'B*ll*cks!'

But eventually, according to Denis Gartside, who was John Kenyon's fellow director on *Gardeners' World* at that time, they developed a good relationship with RAF Cottesmore. 'We would tell them we were filming that day, and they would work around us if they could.' If not, then the team would find out when the pilots were taking their lunch break and get the 'sync' pieces (those involving Geoff talking) done then, and do the close-ups later. On one occasion, no sooner had they got rid of the RAF than a crop-spraying plane came droning over and started buzzing them. Geoff and Denis, armed with a loud-hailer, jumped into a car and set off in pursuit, Denis bellowing ineffectually through the loud-hailer. Geoff said afterwards that if only he'd had a small rocket launcher...

At the beginning, when hardly any of the land was planted up, a bit of cheating sometimes had to go on. Rod Biggs recalls an item on climbing plants, when they had to borrow a number of different varieties from a nurseryman who needed them back after filming. 'We planted them, still in their pots, against a fence and tied them in so that they looked realistic. As soon as the filming was over, they were whisked out again and promptly returned to their owner.' Tony would call him a rogue and a scoundrel for indulging in such devious practices, but Geoff would just smile and carry on.

There were surprisingly few disasters in those early days, although Rod can recall a time when he sprayed an area of rough ground with weedkiller but then forgot to tell anyone that he had done it. 'The crew walked all over the area I'd sprayed and then walked over the lawn. We knew exactly what had happened because three or four days later there were brown footprints right across it! But Geoff didn't get angry about it. He didn't get upset about many things.' In fact, Carol remembers him as relaxed and happy nearly all the time, but he never lost an opportunity to have a little fun with his staff. For example, Carol always made a point of getting to work spot on time, but if Geoff was about when she arrived he would always point dramatically to his watch and say, "What time do you call this, then?"'

When they moved into the new Barnsdale, though, things did change a little because Geoff had made such a huge financial commitment in order to buy it that there was a lot riding on it and so much more pressure to get it right.

One of next areas to be created from the wilderness was the

vegetable trial beds because trials remained a very important element of *Gardeners' World*, helping give the programme its authority. As Geoff wrote in the preface to the *Gardeners' World Vegetable Book*, published in 1981, 'Gardening has never been an exact science. Ask ten good gardeners how they achieve their results and you will almost certainly get ten different answers. And they will all be right! There's no doubt about it, we all have our own pet methods and if they work for us, we are unlikely to change them in a hurry. Controversy always rages and that's one of the factors that makes gardening such a fascinating and absorbing hobby. But when it falls to your lot to advise others seriously, you must at least be as exact as a possible. And that is one of the primary functions of the *Gardeners' World* trial grounds at Barnsdale.'

He went on to say that the aim, given the small gardens most people have these days, was to find ways of getting best use out of the land available and increasing yields. He worked closely with government bodies like the National Vegetable Research Station, and adapted methods that had been developed for commercial growers so that they were suitable for amateur gardeners wherever possible. 'While I feel strongly that hobby gardening should retain much of the traditional methods that make it so enjoyable, there is a lot to be gained from modern technology. And there is no happier gardener than a successful gardener.'

One trial they did very early on was comparing organic methods with inorganic methods, because in those days Geoff, like almost every other gardener in the country, used chemicals and peat. That trial was a particularly significant one, since it was to change the way Geoff gardened for the rest of his life, but more of that in Chapter 7.

The trials were also very important to Geoff because he always believed in passing on to the viewers only information that he had gathered himself and knew from first-hand experience to work. Roy Lancaster, a co-presenter with Geoff on *Gardeners' World* in the

1980s, believes that that was one of the reasons he was so successful. 'He was so much in sympathy with ordinary gardeners because he had faced most of the problems they faced in their own gardens himself. He understood their problems and their aspirations, too, and he knew what could go wrong, so he could always warn or reassure them. While I think he did enjoy experimenting and trying out new methods and new ideas, I was left with the impression that what he loved the most was the basics. He loved sowing seeds, watching them germinate and grow. He loved digging too, he really did. Lots of gardeners get snooty about the basic gardening tasks, but Geoff seemed genuinely to love them, which is why he could do the same jobs year after year on the programme and still convey the same infectious enthusiasm about them.'

When it came to developing Barnsdale, the viewers were upper-most in Geoff's mind. Yes, it was his garden, but it was also the base for *Gardeners' World*. And Geoff knew that the vast majority of the programme's viewers could not relate to a 5-acre garden. So he set about creating a series of small gardens, all of them about the same size of an ordinary garden. 'He didn't sit down with a piece of paper and plan it all out,' Carol says. 'He started up by the house and, as he needed to create a new garden or project for the programme, he just took another piece of land, and over the years worked his way down the garden like that.'

After Versailles came the woodland area. This was where many of the trees Geoff had brought from the first Barnsdale ended up, and, once they were planted, an understorey of shrubs, perennials, ferns and bulbs, all suitable for woodland conditions, were added over a number of years.

He built another version of the £2 a Week Garden – the £4 a Week Garden, which went through a number of changes in its life. In 1989 it became the site for presenter Nigel Colborn's garden, concentrating on herbaceous perennials. 'It was a very odd feeling, working in someone else's garden,' Nigel recalls, 'but Geoff was incredibly generous. He asked me what I wanted, and I said it would be great if the soil could be dug over and organic matter added, and then I'd do the rest, and that was fine with him. He just left me to get on with what I wanted to do.'

In the early 1990s the same garden became the site for Lynda Brown's Cook's Garden, where she grew vegetables with the end use very much in mind, often giving recipe suggestions. This prompted a letter from an irate viewer wanting to know what on earth cooking had got to do with growing vegetables!

Finally, in the autumn after Geoff died, Clare Bradley, best known as the *Blue Peter* gardener, used it to create an all-year-round garden for the daytime series, *Peter Seabrook's Gardening Week*.

Another small garden, which Geoff created in 1984, was called the Garden from Scratch, and it was just that − a bare plot, about the same size as the garden of a two- or three-bedroomed house on a new housing estate. Geoff showed how to make a lawn, lay a patio, plant borders and so on. The Garden from Scratch no longer exists because it was transformed first into the Organic Garden in 1986 and again in 1992 into the Living Garden, used to illustrate the importance of encouraging wildlife into any garden − the philosophy behind the series of the same name which Geoff made in the same year (see Chapter 6).

Other small gardens, too, were built, both for the BBC and, since 1992, for Catalyst Television, the independent company that took over production of *Gardeners' World*.

The Rose Garden, created in the mid-1980s, was designed to show that roses need not be grown in formal rectangular beds with nothing around them but bare soil. Instead, over 50 different varieties − climbing and rambling roses and various types of bush roses − were planted with other climbers and perennials to make a very attractive small garden that was a riot of colour and perfume. Then there was the

Elizabethan Vegetable Garden, with formal deep-beds surrounded by timber edgings and posts, topped by elaborate finials, and designed to be tended from the paths. Additionally, Geoff created a formal knot garden, using box plants he had patiently grown from cuttings, and which is now resplendent with herbs, in the traditional style.

He also designed and built a number of gardens for separate, six-part television series like *The Ornamental Kitchen Garden*, *Geoff Hamilton's Cottage Gardens*, and *Paradise Gardens*, but more about them later.

The last garden Geoff built was the Reclaimed Garden, a replica of the one built at the *Gardeners' World Live* exhibition in 1996. It was a garden close to his heart because it used only recycled materials – second-hand paving, reclaimed timber and, one of its most striking elements, a water feature made from an old copper water tank, carefully crafted to look like a rose. It was two days after Geoff had been filmed putting the water feature in position that he died.

Geoff also created lots of small areas at Barnsdale, either to make a point, to experiment or to offer inspiration. There was the bed for winter colour he planted up with plantsman Adrian Bloom, and an island bed for garden thugs. 'What Geoff wanted to do there,' Nick explains, 'was to bury the myth that plants described as having "an infinite spread" couldn't be used in an average garden. So he planted five notoriously invasive species – *Campanula poscharskyana*, *Campanula takesimana*, *Senecio tanguticus*, *Houttuynia cordata* 'Chameleon' and *Linaria dalmatica* – to see whether they could be contained, and also to let them fight it out because he was curious to see which was the biggest thug of all. The reason it was an island bed, surrounded by grass, was that any escaping shoots would be regularly cut off by the mower, keeping them under control. It worked! Nothing has ever escaped from the bed, and so far the *Senecio* seems to be the winner.'

Water features were always popular. The original pond and bog garden, built in 1986, were shown many times throughout the years, while the pond and stream, built for the 1995 series, were also very popular, showing you could get quite a decent length of stream into a small garden. The idea came from the series producer at the time, Laurence Vulliamy. The stream was one of the most difficult things Geoff had attempted because it involved almost civil engineering to ensure the stream was level, since water will not run uphill. They had filmed all the processes and were very close to finishing when Laurence had a phone call late one night from a very worried Geoff. 'It doesn't work, boy,' he said. The stream appeared to be leaking somewhere, and he couldn't find where. What had happened was that a rock had pushed the liner down a few millimetres too far in one place at the edge so that water was leaking over the top, but it took almost a week to find that out. The thing about Geoff was that he paid so much attention to detail, and if he were going to show the viewers something he had to be 100 per cent certain that it would work.

Tony remembers that when he went to see Geoff one Saturday, on the scrounge for something for his own garden as usual, he had hardly got out of his car when Geoff appeared, grabbed his arm and said, 'Hey, boy, you've just got to come to see my stream.' He was led forcibly through the garden to what appeared to be nothing but a dry bed of small rocks bordered by plants, when Geoff, like the mayor switching on the Blackpool illuminations, threw the switch on the water pump. Suddenly, a trickle of water grew into a burbling stream, pouring triumphantly into his pool. Geoff stood back with a huge smile of achievement on his face.

And then there was the rock garden with the famous home-made rocks, which Geoff started in 1995 in an attempt to persuade people not to use water-worn limestone in their gardens – the main reason for the destruction of the irreplaceable limestone pavements, a cause that became very dear to his heart.

The concrete rocks were made in holes in the ground, lined

roughly with polythene to create natural-looking fissures and then filled with a mixture of coir, cement, sand and cement colouring. As with every project he did, Geoff experimented endlessly first, trying to get the consistency and the colour right, so that when he showed viewers what to do, he would know they'd get the desired result.

Tony, among others, thought Geoff had finally flipped. 'I went up there one day and he said, "Come and look at my concrete rocks." There were a few failed experiments lying around, and he was just about to make what he thought would be the final version. I said, "Come on, Geoff, have you gone daft? That's going to look absolutely terrible. Nobody's going to want to put lumps of concrete in their gardens. You're wasting your time here." And when I first saw the finished product, I said, "I still think it's looks terrible. It's just not going to work." "Oh, ye of little faith," he said, "you just wait until they're embedded in soil and planted up. Then you'll change your mind." And, by golly, he was right. It looks terrific now, and every time I see it I think, "What a clever old devil you were, Geoffrey!"'

One of the joys of working at Barnsdale, as every producer who ever worked there will confirm, was that Geoff was a true professional. He was always flexible and prepared for any eventuality. Whatever he was planning to do would be ready to go, and everything they could possibly need would be on site. If it were a new project, Geoff would have gone through as many dummy runs as he needed to be sure that everything would work on the day.

The team was very small to cope with a 5-acre garden. Rod was responsible for the heavy work and general gardening. Carol, who John Kenyon always says has the greenest fingers he has ever encountered, looked after the greenhouses and much of the propagating, and was also the container queen of Rutland. Lorraine Shone helped out generally, as did Sue Darlington, who was also Geoff's secretary for almost 14 years.

In January 1983 Sue saw an ad in the local paper for a 'secretary-cum-gardener who didn't mind getting her fingernails dirty'. She told Geoff at the interview that she bit her nails anyway, so it wasn't a problem. They got on very well, and as usual with people he was fond of, he was rude about her. 'He used to introduce me to people as a useless secretary but a damned good gardener!' A large part of Sue's secretarial work was typing answers to viewers' letters. Initially, Geoff dictated them on to a tape, but later he would either scrawl the gist of the reply in the margin of the letter or, if he were feeling particularly mischievous, just the first letter of each word of the reply and leave Sue to figure it out. And did they get some letters! The most memorable one that Tony remembers came with a small dead stick enclosed. It said 'Dear Geoff, Is this plant dead? I think I have killed it by overfeeding. I say this because I once had some goldfish that I killed by overfeeding. Have I done the same to this plant?' Geoff was at a loss to know how to reply, but his mischievous sense of humour didn't desert him. He wrote, 'Goldfish generally don't need a lot of food – but they do need a plentiful supply of water!'

The format of *Gardeners' World* remained the same until 1990 – one whole programme coming from Barnsdale one week, with Geoff and a variety of other presenters, and the following two weeks the programme would come from a different garden somewhere, again with a variety of presenters.

The Barnsdale programmes were recorded on Tuesday and Wednesday to go out the following Friday, because John Kenyon felt it was crucial that the programme should be as topical as possible. He might have a rough idea of what would be in that week's programme, but, gardening being what it is, you can never be certain. They may have planned an item on pruning shrubs after flowering, but when the time came to film the programme, the flowers might still be looking so good that it would be perverse to prune then. So the team would arrive on Monday night and walk round the garden to have a good look. Then on Tuesday morning, around the table in Geoff's kitchen, they would sort out exactly what they were doing, how long each item would be, and in what order the items would feature in the programme.

Even then, the British weather could catch them out. Mark Ker-shaw, who became producer in 1988, remembers one occasion very well. 'We'd started on the Tuesday afternoon, and we were shooting the items in the order they would be transmitted. So we'd recorded Geoff's opening piece to camera, and had done some good items, such as getting the lawn ready for summer. By late afternoon we'd done well over half the programme, but the light was going a bit and, since we had all of Wednesday, we decided to stop. Overnight, however, it snowed, so we had to scrap everything we had done, reinvent the programme with items that could all be done in snow, and start all over again.'

On another occasion they had started the programme on the Tuesday in full sun and had ended with Geoff finishing a job in the garden and saying, 'What we need to do now is get this into the greenhouse.' On the Wednesday morning it was bucketing down with rain, and Geoff came into the greenhouse commenting, with a twinkle in his eye, on how suddenly the British weather can change.

Two weeks out of three, the team would visit different gardens all over the country, many of them large and famous, like Hidcote Manor and Abbotsbury. But the type of garden they could visit changed over the years, largely because the technology changed and cameras became smaller and lighter, so they could go to much smaller gardens, though initially the gardens still had to be large enough to sustain a half-hour programme.

Geoff thoroughly enjoyed visiting other gardens, always ready to learn from seeing how other gardeners did things, and finding plants and plant combinations that were entirely new to him. These visits were not always without their problems and dramas, though. On one occasion Denis Gartside, the director on the day, recalls, Geoff was visiting a herb garden in the Midlands and interviewing the owner. The morning had gone extremely well, and the owner had been articulate and interesting. But when the production team went for lunch, he chose not to go with them but with the riggers, who were known for their capacity to hold their liquor. He unfortunately didn't have the same capacity, and when they all got back after lunch ready to start making a window box for herbs, he was extremely belligerent and kept trying to push Geoff out of the way. While Denis Gartside was screaming blue murder in the scanner (the mobile control room), the floor manager, who was hearing all this through headphones, translated it as, 'The director thinks it's better if only one person does this.' The owner said, 'Right, I'll do it,' and shoved Geoff even harder out of the way. In the end he was led gently away.

While the team travelled all over the country, they didn't go abroad much because budgets didn't allow it and, besides, as Geoff knew, *Gardeners' World*'s viewers weren't very interested in abroad unless it related directly to their experience. In the winter of 1985, though, they went to New Zealand – Geoff, John Kenyon and the programme's organizational rock, Jean Laughton, who had been the production assistant for many years. It was a great trip, Jean remembers, with an abundance of good stories to film and some memorable events to brighten the day. She remembers one particular incident vividly. Geoff had left something behind on one location and John Kenyon kept lecturing him throughout the trip about the secret of success being good organization. Then, at the very next stop, John left his briefcase, with all the notes for filming and all the travel details, open on the top of the hire car and drove off. 'So there were Geoff and I chasing down the road like mad butterfly hunters, trying to catch all these flying sheets of paper – while John drove blithely on, unaware of the havoc he had caused!'

New Zealand was a very significant trip for Geoff in other ways too. 'Although we had known each other for almost five years,' Lynda said, 'it was only after he came back that we decided we wanted to be together.' She doesn't remember how he proposed, or whether he even did, but he certainly wasn't the type to go down on one knee, except afterwards as a joke. 'I do remember him saying, "I shall come into the kitchen in my muddy boots. I won't go on the sitting-room carpet in them, but I shall come into the kitchen, so…" Those were the terms, take or leave it!'

They were married one Monday morning before Christmas at the local register office. Since they had both been married before, they didn't want any fuss. 'We didn't need a big wedding and all its attendant trimmings. We just wanted the marriage certificate, that's all. I suppose we both felt we just wanted to make a commitment to each other.'

They certainly didn't want any publicity, so Geoff sent Lynda to get the licence in case he was recognized. 'It was just us, the two witnesses, Tony and Geoff's youngest son Chris, the female registrar and her assistant. It's all so quick that we had to hang around after-wards while they did all the form-filling and so on. And the registrar said, "It may be very quick, but it's still a solemn occasion. After all, getting married isn't fun!" And we thought, oh, that's a disappoint-ment. We thought it was supposed to be fun!'

Afterwards there was lunch at the Noel Arms, the mother and father of all parties for the family in the evening, and what purported to be a genteel drinks party for friends in the New Year. In fact, Geoff didn't have any genteel friends, so it was a similar riot of fun and laughter.

On the surface they seemed an unlikely pair. Lynda was a softly spoken, university-educated (which went down very well with Rosie) language teacher at a public school, and Geoff was none of those things. But, as Lynda says, they had more in common than people thought. She was a country girl, born and brought up in the neighbouring county of Leicestershire, and part of a large extended family who were farmers and gardeners. And they also complemented each other. Geoff was the outgoing extrovert, driven ceaselessly by boundless nervous energy, who gave Lynda strength and restored her self-confidence. 'When a relationship has gone sour, you do put up lots of barriers, and it's a long time before you think you will trust anyone else. But I did feel confident with Geoff because he was warm, fun and adventurous.'

Lynda, the calmer, quieter one, came to be his anchor, and people who knew them well had no doubt that in Lynda Geoff had found what he needed. 'Although Geoff was the life and soul of any party,' Fay Howison says, 'always incredibly popular so that everyone wanted to be in Geoff's gang, as it were, I always felt there was a slight hollowness at the centre. After he and Lynda got together, he seemed so much more at peace with himself. I had often wondered whether he would ever settle down, but he took to domesticity like a duck to water.'

Lynda was surprised too. In the years before they were married Geoff used to go down to the pub most nights, at 10 o'clock when he had been at home all evening writing, for fear that he was missing out on the fun. After they were married he became a home body and didn't want to go out much any more. He was never comfortable in other people's houses, Lynda remembers, and certainly didn't like staying the night. Chris recalls that in four years Geoff came to his home only twice. The first time he and Catherine, his wife, were out walking the dogs and came back to find a note on the kitchen table from Geoff saying, 'Came in. No one home. Had a pee. Left.' Geoff didn't usually tell people he was coming, perhaps because he wanted to surprise them, or perhaps because there was always the chance they wouldn't be in, and so he would get the Brownie points for coming without actually having to go through with a visit.

The fact that he preferred to be in his own home did not mean that he became remotely interested in the house itself. As long as he had a good fire, some pictures and his books and his records, he was happy. 'He liked some chairs we bought because they were hand-made and functional. But he hated anything like draped curtains – as far as he was concerned, curtains were to keep the dark out.'

Lynda was surprised, too, that although Geoff was still great fun, and laughter is the thing that she misses most now, he had a more serious side to him than she had expected. He was also far less chaotic than she thought he was. Although he appeared to be a mess, he actually knew where everything was and was quite systematic about things. And he lived to quite a strict timetable. He wasn't an early riser. He'd wake at about 8 and stay in bed for an hour or so thinking about things he needed to do. After breakfast, he would read the *Guardian* and be out in the garden by 10. He might come in for coffee mid-morning, or sometimes Lynda would take it out to him, and then lunch was at 1. Back into the garden for another two hours, then into his office in one of the barns next to the house at 4 to catch up on let-ters and phone calls and if possible get on with some writing. He watched the news at 6 p.m and again at 7, with dinner in between, and then from 8 to 10 o'clock he'd be back in his office writing.

The exceptions were Mondays – singing in the evening with the Oakham Choral Society, which the former members of the Exton Singers had joined – and Fridays, when they would watch *Gardeners' World* and then go out for a meal at a restaurant. Chris, who lived with Geoff and Lynda for a time remembers the venue always being a matter for debate. 'The old man would say, "What do you fancy? Chinese or Indian?" and I'd say, "I don't mind. You choose." He'd say, "No. I don't mind either – you choose. Indian or Chinese?" I'd say, "Chinese would be nice. Or Indian." "OK, Indian then. Or what about a pizza?" Long after I'd moved out, he and Lynda used to have the same discussion on a Friday night, and the old man would say, "Shall we ring Chris and ask him what we should have?"'

When Geoff and Lynda married, her two sons Jeremy and William were living with their father not far away, though since they were at Oakham School, Lynda saw them most days and they spent weekends at Barnsdale. 'They often talked about school, and when Geoff had had enough, he would say, "And how *is* Carruthers today?" and they'd know it was time to change the subject! Geoff handled my "chaps", as he called them, lightly. He was mindful of the fact that they already had a father and treated them as good mates.'

Despite the fact that his own three boys lived with their mother after she and Geoff were divorced, Geoff was able to maintain a good relationship with them all, to such an extent that two of the three wound up working with him at Barnsdale. Chris was the one who got away, although Geoff was instrumental in helping him decide what he wanted to do. He was at art college doing fine art, and pottery was very much a subsidiary subject. Geoff had a friend in Oakham, Dick Clarke, who was a potter and who owned an art gallery in the town. 'He told him that I wanted to be a potter – which I didn't; I wanted to starve in a garret somewhere – and that I'd love to work for him in the summer holidays. He told me about it *after* he'd fixed it up. He thought I was aimless, and he didn't like aimlessness. I moaned like hell at first because it was an 8-mile bike ride to get there, up steep hills, but within a couple of weeks I was hooked. I was a potter.'

Geoff encouraged him, but Chris never knew that he was proud of what he did until the day Geoff and Lynda called in at the museum in Stoke-on-Trent, where he was working, demonstrating throwing on the wheel. 'Lynda told me afterwards that on the way home he couldn't stop talking about it and about how good he thought I was. He never said anything to me himself, of course. That wasn't his way. He never told me that he loved me, either. I know he did, but he would never say anything like that. The Hamiltons didn't go in for that sort of emotional display, and he always said the trouble with me was that I was too emotional and sensitive! But he'd show it in his own way. He bought me my first kiln – an expensive piece of kit I don't think he could afford – and then badgered me endlessly to make flowerpots and containers that he would sell for me in the nursery. He would talk to me on the phone for hours, because I lived a long way away and didn't see him too much and – the greatest delight of all – he adored my wife Catherine. A man of good taste as well.'

As for Stephen, Geoff had already successfully dealt with his perceived aimlessness some years earlier. After he had dropped out of college, he had been living on the dole, playing music and having a great time. Geoff was still writing for *Practical Gardening* and taking his own photographs, so he suggested that Stephen might like to do the photographs instead. 'So I did, and sold a few, but then I thought if I'm going to do this, I ought to learn how to do it properly. So I wrote to every photographer within a 25-mile radius offering to come and work for nothing, and I got one reply! And I really fell on my feet because not only was he a really nice bloke, but a very good commercial photographer. I took my earring out when I went for the interview – the old man's words had gone deep – and he said I needn't have bothered, but he appreciated me making the effort. He offered to pay my petrol money to and from the studio, and I was in. I learnt so much from him.'

He then set up a studio in another of the barns at Barnsdale and began working with Geoff, taking photographs for the many magazine articles and books that Geoff wrote. But while Stephen is very conscious that working with Geoff really kick-started his career and gave him contacts that would otherwise have taken him many years to build up, there was also a downside. 'Working with him was a nightmare some of the time. I suppose the closest analogy is having your father teach you to drive! Because we were related, he was in a position to complain a lot, and so he blooming well did. "Come on," he'd say, "get on with it. I haven't got all day! Other photographers don't take this long!" Of course they did. They took longer because he wouldn't dare treat them like he treated me. I was constantly trying to slow him down, so that we'd get the best shots, or I'd ask him to change his jumper because it didn't look quite right, but it was always a battle.

'He used to try to tell me how to do my job sometimes. He'd say, "You want to get a shot of that group of plants over there," and I'd say, "No, the light's terrible!" and he'd say, "No, it's not, it's good. Take it, go on, take it." And so I'd have to take it, and then I'd take it again the next day when the light was much better and show him the two shots.' Stephen doesn't think that Geoff was a control freak, wanting to run his sons' lives. 'If asked, he'd say that was the very last thing he wanted to do. I think it was more that he wanted to look after us all, and make sure we would do all right. I'm not sure that he entirely trusted us to do it on our own.'

Of all his sons, Nick was always the most likely to end up working with Geoff since he had followed him into horticulture. In 1990 the perfect opportunity arose. Geoff decided to borrow the money to acquire another piece of land next to the garden and set up the business he should always have had – a nursery specializing in unusual plants. And who better to run it than Nick? He had absolutely no qualms about working with Geoff. 'We worked together very well. Obviously, I knew the kind of things he expected, and he knew what I was about and the sort of place I wanted to make it. He had his input, but he left it very much to me, and kept telling me he was only popping down here to keep an eye on his investment! He'd make the odd comment sometimes, but it was always helpful, never negative, so I never had any problems with that at all. One of the things about horticulture is that you never stop learning. I never stopped learning from him, and he never stopped learning from everybody else, so in that respect we were both in the same position.'

For the first year Nick helped in the garden as well as working on the site growing the plants they would sell, laying out the nursery and putting up the small wooden building that would serve as the shop. Barnsdale Plants opened in 1991 on the Whitsun Bank Holiday weekend, with just one and a half display beds. The first mail-order catalogue had just 316 varieties; the most recent has nearly 1500.

One thing that didn't change was Geoff's head for business – or lack of one. Nick would tell him that they really needed to buy something for the nursery or get a job done, and Geoff would say, 'We're all right for money at the moment, so go ahead.' 'He never seemed to grasp the fact that in business you get something done or buy something and then get billed for it a month or so later. So the bill would come in, I'd take it to him in the office and say, "This needs paying," and he'd explode! "What have you spent that kind of money for?" I'd remind him that he'd told me to go ahead last month. He'd say, "Well, yes, but that was then. I've got no money now!"'

The business was very slow to get off the ground, in part because Geoff was absolutely scrupulous about not using his position with the BBC to promote it, perhaps mindful of the fate of Percy Thrower, who was fired when he started advertising gardening products, but also because Geoff's own sense of what was right and wrong told him that he shouldn't do it. Over the years many viewers had asked to be allowed to visit Barnsdale, but of course this just wasn't practical, because the gardens always had to be in perfect condition for the cameras, and with thousands of feet walking over the lawns that would have been impossible. But Geoff hit on the idea of re-creating some of the television gardens in the nursery to make it more of a draw for potential visitors looking for an afternoon out, and so Barnsdale Plants and Gardens was born.

In 1990 Geoff had placed an advertisement in the trade paper

Horticulture Week for a young landscaper. Among the many that saw it was Adam Frost, whose father Martin had worked with Geoff when he had his landscaping business nearly 30 years before. 'I knew who he was, but I hadn't seen him on television then – when you're in the trade you tend not to watch gardening programmes – so when I got an interview I thought I'd better watch a few. When I met him, he was just what I'd expected from the television – very friendly, easy-going, jokey. He was also generous – I'd driven up from London for the interview, and he wouldn't let me leave without giving me petrol money and something to cover my lunch.'

Adam didn't really expect to get the job. When Geoff rang him a few weeks later and offered it to him, he was so surprised that all he could say was, 'Oh. Right.' But Tony knows why he got the job. Geoff said to him, 'If he's as good as his dad was, then he's the man for me. Anyway, with our old relationship, he's practically family.'

Over the next six years Adam worked with Geoff designing and building gardens for his *Cottage Gardens* series, the Town Garden for the *Paradise Gardens* series – Geoff designed the country one himself – the Parterre Garden and the Reclaimed Garden, as well as number of smaller projects. Like many of the people who have worked for Geoff over the years, Adam felt he wasn't like a boss at all. 'His way was always to be rude to me in a jokey way and make me the butt of jokes, but he could take it as well as dish it out, so I would be rude back. What I really liked was that I was allowed not to agree with his principles and ideas, and we had words over the years, even a couple of rows. Sometimes in the end he would say, "Well, I'm the boss, and we'll do it my way," but not that often. What he would never say was, "OK, I'm wrong and you're right," but sometimes he would just mutter, "Whatever…" and wander off, and you knew you were free to do it your way. Having worked with Nick and Stephen very closely, I know it's a Hamilton trait to be reluctant to admit they're wrong.'

They argued about garden design. Geoff had paid for Adam to do a year's course with David Stevens at Capel Manor, so what Adam liked doing was designing and building gardens and believed the structure was a very important part, while Geoff liked filling every available space with plants. 'Getting too much like Stevens, you are!' he would mutter to Adam sometimes. If he saw a foot or two of bare soil, even though the shrubs around it would easily fill it by the end of the season, he would plant something in it, despite Adam pointing out that they would have to dig it out the following year.

They also argued about colour. Geoff's view was that you should throw everything in together this year and if it looked awful you could always move the plants next year. '"A nice splash of colour," was one of Geoff's favourite phrases and one I came to dread. I just think he loved plants, and I don't think it mattered to him too much what they looked like together.'

My own experience of working with Geoff bears that out. On the first series we did together of *First Time Garden* in 1988 (see Chapter 6), there was a small bed for a climber on the patio, which was to be underplanted with bedding. Geoff had put in magenta pelargoniums with bright orange marigolds, and the result, in my view anyway, was serious damage to the optic nerve. While he was off doing some-thing else, I replaced them with tasteful pastels – pale blues, pinks and whites. Nothing was said, but I noticed some time later the magenta and orange were back. 'That's what you want,' Geoff said, with a twinkle in his eye. 'A nice splash of colour!'

According to Adam, Geoff was usually quicker to criticize than he was to praise – at least to his face – though he learnt that Geoff was much more generous with compliments about him when he wasn't around. 'When we did the Reclaimed Garden at *Gardeners' World Live* in 1996, Geoff had left it pretty much to me. I had charge of the budget and basically just got on with it. The morning of the opening, he put his arm round my shoulders and said, "It's fantastic. I never thought it would be this good!" That was the first time he had ever put his arm round me, and it really choked me up. I was going on holiday the following week, and after we had won a Silver Gilt Medal for the garden he pushed £1000 into my hand and said, "Here you are. This is for doing such a good job." I said, "But it's what you pay me to do!" and he said, "No, take it, and have a good holiday." '

As well as paying a good deal better than most people in the horticultural industry, Geoff was also very generous to his staff in other ways. When Adam and his girlfriend at the time were splitting up and he wasn't sure of what would happen to the house they were buying, Geoff called him into the office and said, 'Whatever happens, don't lose the house. You must keep it even if I have to pay the mortgage for six months. I want you to stay around.'

And just before he died, Geoff made Adam an offer. If he carried on working at Barnsdale for another two years, Geoff would then set him up in his own design and landscaping business. 'You'd be part of my pension,' he said, 'because I'll take 10 per cent.' Adam has now set up in business for himself, though he still works at Barnsdale sometimes. He is enormously grateful for his time with Geoff and learnt a lot from him. 'He was brilliant at getting on with all kinds of people at all levels. I used to worry about my accent when I was speaking to wealthy people, but Geoff hung on to his, and from seeing how he operated I've learnt to believe in myself.'

Shortly before Adam arrived at Barnsdale, Geoff had placed another advert in *Horticulture Week*, this time for a kitchen gardener. Ian Spence, who became a very familiar face helping Geoff on the programme when he needed an extra pair of hands and appearing in many photographs, was the lucky candidate.

Soon after Ian arrived in 1989, Rod left because for personal reasons he had to move out of the area. So at the beginning of 1990 Ian became head gardener, and his sense of humour was put to the test as his Scottish accent soon became a butt for Geoff's jokes. He worked very closely with Geoff for seven years and has enormous admiration for him as a very good practical gardener who just happened to be on television. He also admired the fact that Geoff remained down to earth and without pretensions, despite his success. He was working in the garden one day when Geoff came by in dirty jeans and muddy boots, as usual. 'I'm off to see the bank manager,' he said. 'Should I change my clothes?' Then, without waiting for Ian to reply, went on, 'Sod it! Why should I? He'll be in his working clothes!'

Geoff had always planned to open the gardens to the public once he had retired from television. After his death in August 1996, Nick, to whom Geoff left the nursery and the main gardens, had no doubt that it was the right thing to do. 'I could have quite comfortably shut the door and said, "Right, he left the garden to me, and I just want to keep it as his. I don't want people spoiling it." But I know for a fact he wouldn't have wanted that, and I certainly don't think it would have been fair not to allow people to come to see it and share it. There are very few people who depart this world leaving something so wonderful for people to enjoy.'

The gardens opened to the public at Easter 1997 and, as Nick had predicted, 60,000 people visited in the first year. What he hadn't predicted, though, was their reaction. 'They come out of the garden and they are totally mixed up. On the one hand they are elated to have seen the garden, but on the other they're very sad, some of them in tears, and all they want to talk about is him. That's helped me a lot emotionally.' The first year, they were feeling their way rather, working to turn what had been a rather higgledy-piggledy collection of small gardens designed specifically for television into a satisfying whole. But in 1998 the gardens looked better than they ever did in Geoff's day because then they concentrated on the areas that were being filmed, and inevitably with such a small staff they couldn't keep the whole garden up to scratch. Nick has absolutely no problems in keeping the garden as Geoff would have wanted it since he admired enormously what Geoff had achieved and doesn't feel in any way constrained because their thoughts on gardening were almost identical. 'I do tell people that I am very much my own person, but I am very like him, and in his own way he moulded me into a mini-Geoff.'

Like Lynda, Nick has a very strong sense of Geoff still in the garden, especially in the early mornings or in the evenings when the visitors have gone and he almost expects to see him coming round a corner. He loved the place so much that he wanted to be buried there, but, as Nick says, that just wasn't practical. The gardens have to be run as a business now, and while Nick would fight to the bitter end to keep them, who knows what lies ahead?

In the meantime, Barnsdale continues to attract visitors by the coachload, and, to borrow Sir Christopher Wren's words about himself and St Paul's Cathedral, if they seek Geoff's monument, all they need to do is look around.

CHAPTER SIX

THE GREAT COMMUNICATOR

Geoff was not only a great gardener, he also had a great talent for communicating his subject and his enthusiasm for it. Many people started gardening purely because of Geoff, many others became passionate because they became infused (or infected) with *his* passion, and others still have in their gardens features or plants that he first showed them. Geoff had that extraordinary gift of appearing ordinary, just like the rest of us, and giving the impression that if *he* could do something, then so could you. As the broadcaster Henry Kelly once said, Geoff was so clever that you'd be out there in the garden the day after a broadcast, having bought all the bits and having made a start before you realized just how clever he was. Tony speaks of the many people he still meets who tell him of their garden exploits, inspired by Geoff, which may not be as good as he made them look, but without him they would never have existed at all.

He made his audiences in print and on television feel that he was on their side, looking out for their interests, that he knew and understood the problems they faced and the circumstances in which they gardened. That was because in his landscaping business he really had experienced all the problems that a person buying a new house faced. He would get frustrated with his producers and say, 'Look, our audience doesn't live in a stately home. They have 50 square yards of clay and builders' rubble, and they just want to know what the hell to do with it!' That's what he really wanted to do – to pass on his passion to ordinary men or women, the people he really identified with.

Obviously, gardening is tied to the seasons, and the same jobs come up year after year. But even though he had done the same thing many, many times before, Geoff could still sow seeds or prune a rose with a genuine enthusiasm that came leaping out of the screen, because he loved it, believed in it and was desperate to share it with others, so that they would get the same pleasure out of it that he did.

Geoff didn't garden for television. He would have gardened whether or not the cameras were there, and that came across. One of Denis Gartside's abiding memories of Geoff is that as the production team drove away after they'd finished a programme, there would be Geoff walking down the garden to get on with some gardening. As he wrote to his old friend, Marilyn Norvell (née Early) in 1992 about his garden, 'I love it because, after television, it's a bit of real life again. I mustn't complain because I've been very lucky to have been in the right place at the right time, but television people take themselves so seriously that sometimes I just have to get out in the garden and release a few pent-up frustrations.'

While he understood that Barnsdale was a television studio, it was also his garden and he loved having it all to himself. That's why there were never any staff there at weekends. Lynda would do all the watering in the greenhouses, having been instructed in the correct method, of course, and Geoff would do the rest.

There is no doubt that Geoff, like Cyril, was a great salesman when he was talking about something he loved.

As he grew older Geoff developed an enormous personal charm which made him equally popular both with women and men. Women of all ages liked the twinkle in his eye, his laughter lines and his slightly crumpled appearance, while men, far from seeing him as a threat, saw him as the sort of bloke from whom they could easily borrow a hedge trimmer or have a pint with at the local. In fact, on

Saturday morning, when Tony usually went to Barnsdale to scrounge something, he would find the yard packed, shoulder to shoulder, with other friends after bedding plants or fertilizer or the loan of a mower or something else for their garden. Geoff would revel in his good fortune to be in a position to provide for them, and the smile never left his face.

His charm also worked miracles one to one, even with people notoriously resistant to charm, like traffic policemen. Once he was driving through a 30-mph speed limit at 60 and was stopped by a policeman. 'Do you know how fast you were going, sir?' Geoff tapped his speedometer and said, 'I'm sure I was only doing 30, officer.' The policeman said, 'As a matter of fact we have just recorded you doing 59 miles per hour, so I will have to book you.' Geoff said, 'Would it help if I said the British police were the finest in the world?' The policeman said it wouldn't help, no. So Geoff then went into a long routine about how if this had been America he would probably have been shot by now, but thank goodness it was England, with the good old British police...until in the end the policeman said to him, 'Oh, just sod off!' and Geoff drove away. He told the story to Tony, so when Tony was stopped in very similar circumstances some time later, he said, 'Would it help if I said the British police were the finest in the world?' and the policeman said, 'Are you trying to bribe me, sir?' 'No, no,' said Tony quickly. 'Book me, please book me.' As he said afterwards, why was it only Geoff who could get away with that kind of outrageous nonsense?

Geoff's journalistic career started as a freelance writer, and after his in-house stints on *Garden News* and *Practical Gardening* he became a freelance writer again, contributing among other things the 'Last Word' column to *Garden News* for 10 years until he finally gave up in 1991 when he was swamped by other commitments. His editor for some of that time was Adam Pasco, now editor of *Gardeners' World Magazine*. 'I had long admired Geoff, so it was a rather odd experience to find that he was one of my contributors, and just as odd to find myself sitting at his kitchen table drinking coffee.'

Geoff's great talent as a journalist, Adam believes, is that as you read his articles it was as if he were speaking the words to you inside your head. He conveyed the same passion, the same enthusiasm, in the same language as he used when he spoke. 'He wasn't trying to be clever, not trying to be a "writer", just trying to communicate to people as though they had asked for his advice about their garden.'

Nigel Colborn, who worked with Geoff on *Gardeners' World* between 1990 and 1992, believes he also had that other great journalists' gift – the ability to gather knowledge very quickly and retain it. He was then able to muster an argument very clearly and cogently.

From Adam's point of view as an editor, Geoff was an ideal contributor, never late with his copy and never a prima donna if ever Adam had to send a piece back because it wasn't quite right, or to ask him to change it. The 'Last Word' column was meant to be controversial, and Geoff had no difficulty in finding a hobbyhorse to ride each week. Value for money for the ordinary gardener was one of his great crusades, so he would write about the pointlessness of putting a product inside a plastic bag inside a box inside another layer of plastic. Sometimes he would go too far, and Adam would have to ask him to tone it down. '"You can't say that," I'd tell him. "We'll be sued!" And he'd reply, "I thought you'd say that!" But he liked to try it on, just to see.'

Geoff did run into legal problems a couple of times – once over an article he wrote for *Gardeners' World Magazine*, in which he criticized the way in which a trial of organic methods had been conducted by *Gardening Which?*. That was settled without recourse to law when the magazine published a letter from the editor of *Gardening Which?* defending their methodology. The second time was a contretemps with another well-known gardening writer over an article Geoff wrote in *Garden News* concerning peat after he had stopped using it for environmental reasons. Again the matter was settled out of court. 'That upset him tremendously,' Lynda recalls, 'because he couldn't bear it if there was ill feeling. He wanted to be in accord with everybody.'

In the spring of 1989 Geoff was invited to become the *Radio Times* gardening columnist, something that pleased him enormously. His editor in the first few years with *Radio Times* was Catherine Fenton, who found him a dream to work with. 'Unlike a lot of experts, Geoff was also a very good writer, and he had such a distinctive style that I edited his copy as little as possible. And when I did he never, ever complained. Not a trace of the prima donna about him at all.' He was also 100 per cent reliable, always getting his copy in on time regardless of the circumstances. Once, when he was suffering from a recurring back problem and was unable to move, he dictated it down the phone to her, lying on the sitting-room floor. His gift as a journalist, Catherine felt, was that he had that common touch. He was very good at explaining things simply, but you could always read his copy on several levels. There was something in it for the beginner and something for the more experienced gardener. He didn't exclude anyone, and that is a difficult trick to pull off. Working with him had such a lasting impact on her that she is now a keen gardener – to the extent that at one point she considered retraining for a career in horticulture.

While Geoff was delighted to be the *Radio Times* gardening correspondent, he felt that what he really would like, to complete the set as it were, was a national newspaper column. In the spring of 1991 he got his wish when the *Daily Express* approached him and asked him to be their gardening correspondent. From the paper's point of view he was a dream contributor – always on time with copy, and if, on a Thursday night when they were working on Saturday's feature pages, they suddenly found they had lost an advert and needed more words, they knew they could ring Geoff and he would provide the additional text almost at once. 'He was a real pro,' said Roger Watkins of the features department, 'providing good, clean copy that needed hardly anything doing to it, and the readers loved him.' They may have thought they did very little to Geoff's copy, but there were a few Saturday mornings when he opened the *Express* to read his page and spotted an error – the 'i' wrongly placed in 'aub-rieta' was one that exercised him – and suddenly the paper would be flying across the kitchen, accompanied by his favourite expletive.

The money the *Express* paid Geoff enabled him to employ Adam Frost to do all the landscaping at Barnsdale, and he often used to comment on the irony of having to sit in his office writing to pay someone to do the job he would have loved to do himself.

Also in 1991, Geoff was invited to contribute a page called 'Down to Earth' once a month to the magazine *Country Living*. One of his editors there was Paula McWaters. 'I think Geoff viewed our readers with a healthy cynicism at first because he felt they all had masses of money to throw around, but of course they didn't. They loved him, though. When we did some reader research we found that his page was one of the most popular features in the magazine.'

Geoff used to say jokingly that one page really wasn't enough and that they ought to give him more, though with all his other commit-ments, which also included regular monthly articles for *Gardeners' World Magazine* from 1992 onwards, it's hard to know quite when he would have found the time to fill them.

But it was on television that Geoff found his perfect means of communication. While he always fiercely resisted any suggestion that he was a television personality, and maintained he was just an ordi-nary bloke who gardened, he was undoubtedly a natural performer, as indicated by his almost unbroken succession of singing and acting from the church choir at seven, via gang shows and college concerts to the Exton Singers at forty-seven. But communicating one to one was what he did best. He was very lucky, though, to encounter at the start of his main broadcasting career a producer like John Kenyon, who taught him how to communicate with people individually in their own living-rooms, rather than with an audience, and who helped him to find the way of conveying information very clearly without appearing to teach. 'From the very beginning, I didn't want Geoff standing and talking about what he had done or what he was going to do. I wanted him doing and talking whenever possible, so it would be digging or weeding or pruning, bending his back and getting his hands dirty. And Geoff always wanted to be doing. He was essentially a practical man, and was very proud of being practical.'

He was also very professional, and when he realized that he no longer had enough breath to dig and talk, he gave up smoking on the spot. 'From having been a smoker since his days in the RAF,' Lynda recalls, 'and smoking full-strength cigarettes, too, he stopped just like that. He thought, my job's on the line here, and so he gave it up. He had tremendous willpower. It was the same with drinking. He could really knock back the gin at one time, but when he realized that he was putting on the inches round his waistline, he gave that up too. He'd heard that red wine was good for you, so that's what he drank, red wine and occasionally Ruddles County, now sadly threatened by the brewery's new owners.'

Geoff also learnt early on the benefits of being well prepared for the items he had to do on camera. John Kenyon recalls a programme from Powis Castle where Geoff was showing how to train an apple tree. 'He ended up with bits of string everywhere and got himself into the most tremendous muddle, which only went to teach him how important it was to prepare himself thoroughly.'

He was a very fast learner, as another item Geoff did a year or so later clearly showed. He was making a hypertufa trough using, typically, a cardboard box for a mould and bits of chicken wire to make a skeleton for the hypertufa mixture of cement, sand and coir. It was a very tricky operation, with plenty of opportunities for things to go wrong, but Geoff did the whole six-and-a-half-minute piece in one take. It's the only time John Kenyon had ever seen a film crew stand back and applaud.

Like all *Gardeners' World* presenters, Geoff was never given a script, and he never actually sat down and wrote out what he was going to say either. He knew the points he wanted to cover and in what order they should come. Then he would say, 'Just give me a few minutes to get my head together,' and he would go off by himself, pacing up and down or round in circles, eyes on the ground, lips moving as he went through his words. People who worked closely with him knew that this was never a good time to interrupt him. Then he'd come back and he would do the piece, and more often than not he would get it right first time.

Nigel Colborn remembers with awe watching Geoff do a long piece to camera in the ornamental kitchen garden. There was a technical problem right at the end, so they had to do it again, and the second performance was almost identical to the first, only very slightly more polished. If there were a good practical or editorial reason for something being done over and over again, then Geoff was endlessly patient. If he didn't feel there was a good reason, or he felt people were trying to tinker with his words unnecessarily, then he would question it and fight his corner, but he very rarely lost his temper.

At one stage in the mid-1980s the programme was made by a process called Editeching, which meant that it was done in the order in which it would go out and recorded directly on to the transmission tape, so the production team would know to the second how much time was left at the end for Geoff's final tip, the trails for the following week's programme and his goodbye. As he did the piece, the floor manager would be counting him down, and he would always come out exactly to time or with just a second or two to spare.

On another occasion, in the winter of 1995, the production team arrived at Barnsdale and found there'd been a heavy fall of snow. As

Betty Talks, the producer at the time, recalls, Geoff felt they should all simply turn round again and go home. 'Geoff was always very reluctant to do anything that he felt real gardeners just wouldn't do, and he felt that no proper gardener would walk about in his garden when there was snow on the ground. In the end we persuaded him to do his opening piece, walking through the virgin snow in the woods near the house. We only had one crack at it because once it had been walked on, the effect would have been spoilt. Geoff did it perfectly first time, and it made a magical opening to the programme.'

Mind you, he didn't always get things right. Tony remembers with glee the time he was showing viewers how to sow grass seed. He had a part of the plot marked out with string and was bending, feet apart, broadcasting the seed. He then said, 'Of course, you won't have to mark out the whole lawn. You'll soon get used to spreading the seed over a square yard. After all, as you can see, I've got a yard between my legs!' He got a standing ovation when he walked into the pub that night!

But Geoff wasn't just a technically proficient presenter. He also had a very special relationship with the camera, able to communicate on a very personal level. He was able to make every viewer feel that he was talking only to him or her, as was proved after he died by the huge number of people who had never met him who either wrote or phoned the BBC to say they felt they had lost a member of their family.

Liz Rigbey, who worked with Geoff on *Gardeners' World* between 1992 and 1994, admired the real rapport Geoff had with the camera. 'He saw it as his route to the viewer, and he really cared about the viewers.'

Before *Gardeners' World* changed its format in 1990 and became a magazine programme with filmed inserts linked by segments done from Barnsdale each week, Geoff used to go visiting other gardens. Mark Kershaw, who joined the programme as a producer in 1991, was impressed not only with Geoff's natural style with all kinds of people, whether they lived in a stately home or a council house, but also with how good he was at putting them at their ease.

Francesca Kay looks after the medieval garden at Tretower in Wales, and it was she, famously, who got Geoff to go down on one knee in *Paradise Gardens* and say something romantic to her as part of her explanation of medieval courtly love. 'I had the most wonderful day with Geoff. We just sat in the garden and chatted. He asked lots of questions, offered lots of opinions and was really interested to discuss things. He was also very generous as an interviewer, and gave you the time and space to speak. I have done several other bits of television since, and I haven't found the same generosity in anyone else.' The day had a more profound effect on Francesca than she realized. She gives lots of talks on the medieval garden, and it was only when someone who had been to a previous talk asked her recently why she didn't do the bit about courtly love any more that she realized she hadn't done it since Geoff died. 'It would have felt disrespectful somehow, not appropriate any more.'

Geoff also worked with a number of other presenters over the years, both at Barnsdale and on the garden visits. 'I think perhaps there were small jealousies in the early years,' John Kenyon says, 'when the others got to do the exciting stuff while Geoff did the vegetables. But he understood why it had to be that way.'

Roy Lancaster was very careful not to tread on Geoff's toes when he started on the programme. 'I was sure he would be wondering how I was going to fit in, so I said to him very early on that I was there as a plantsman, not a gardener, and there was no way I wanted to be doing any of the things he was doing. He seemed happy with that.' Roy admired Geoff enormously and feels he learnt a great deal from him about being a gardening presenter. 'He looked at plants in a completely different way from the way I did then. I would explain where a plant was first collected and by whom, and what it was like in its natural habitat, and Geoff would say to me, "That's all well and good, Roy, but can I grow it in my garden?" I was only telling half the story, if you like, and Geoff taught me how to tell the full story.'

Roy says another valuable quality he learnt from Geoff was humility. 'When you're young you think you know it all. I had a lot of knowledge about plant history and the correct names and so on, and so when the production team told me they wanted to get everything right, I took them at their word. I was in the scanner one day when Geoff was doing a piece with someone who called a plant by the wrong name. Without thinking, I said, "That's not so and so, it's such and such." Immediately, John Kenyon said into the floor manager's earpiece, "Tell Geoff Roy says he's got that wrong." I felt dreadful, and I heard Geoff say, "Oh, bloody hell! He's not in the scanner, is he?" and then he said, "The man who's growing it calls it so and so, so let's go with that, shall we?" And of course he was right. From then on I always took the view that if someone you're interviewing calls a plant by an incorrect name, then better to let it go and put the correct name in the caption on screen afterwards than risk embarrassing them by correcting them on air.'

Roy believes that for someone as successful and popular as Geoff, he displayed remarkably little ego and was always very generous to other presenters. He remembers a time when they were going to film in a garden in Dorset and had been walking round first, deciding who would cover what. In an area they'd agreed Roy was going to do, Geoff suddenly spotted a plant that he really wanted to talk about because it brought back all sorts of happy memories from childhood days. So Roy rejigged his piece and Geoff talked very poignantly about those memories. That night in the pub, he apologized to Roy. 'I said, "What for?" He said, "I know I mucked up your piece. I've never done that before, and I won't do it again." It was his show, he was the main presenter, and he could do what he liked, and most people in his position wouldn't have given it a second thought, let alone apologized for it.'

When whole programmes came from Barnsdale, Geoff found himself in the rather odd position of having other presenters coming and working in his garden. Pippa Greenwood, who joined the team in 1989, was very nervous the first time she had to do any practical work in Geoff's garden. 'I was doing an item on rose problems and a new product that had been launched. Because I was new I needed lots and lots of takes to get it right, so there I was trampling all over his border and compressing his soil. Afterwards I felt very guilty and tried discreetly to fluff it up with a fork, but he caught me at it, put an arm round my shoulder and said, "Don't worry. You don't have to do that."'

Geoff always seemed to sense when she was floundering internally and would offer support or advice, but he never pushed it. She admired his talent for presenting information very simply, without ever appearing to be condescending or patronizing, and his ability to make eye contact with the camera and make it feel one to one. She also learnt a few useful tricks from watching him at work. 'He was a classic pacer when he was preparing to do a piece to camera, and I soon realized that's a very good way of getting away from people when you need some space without appearing to be rude.' Like many of the people who worked with him, Pippa saw Geoff very much as a mentor, someone she could ring up for help and advice, and someone who would occasionally ring her up with a discreet word in her ear.

In 1991 the government decreed that 25 per cent of all BBC programmes had to be made by independent production companies, and the contract to make *Gardeners' World* went to Catalyst Television. Geoff rang Pippa and, having ascertained that she hadn't introduced herself to them yet, told her that she should. 'He used to remind me that I had something to offer. I think perhaps early on in his career he felt he had undervalued his own worth, so he was very keen that younger people shouldn't make the same mistake.'

Anne Swithinbank, who had joined the team two years earlier, was also very grateful to Geoff for his support and advice. She had come from a very straight horticultural background – parks department, the Royal Botanic Gardens at Kew, the RHS's garden at Wisley – and had been taught to garden by the book. And that's how she started on the programme. 'Geoff used to laugh at the rather grand way I wanted to do things, with mounds of compost and endless terracotta pots, and he'd say, "What about the people with very small back gardens and no money?" I was very young then, so I did feel that my professionalism was being challenged a bit. Once I'd left Wisley and started to garden like everybody else, I understood exactly what he meant.'

Over the years Geoff worked with many different producers and under different regimes, so it was inevitable that he wouldn't always see eye to eye with all of them. There was a campaign in the late 1980s to smarten up all the *Gardeners' World* presenters. With the man who took great pride in having been once voted the worst dressed man on television and who used to claim that Central Wool Growers in Stamford – purveyors of checked shirts and jumpers with elbow patches to the farming community – were his tailors, they were on a hiding to nothing. Geoff had very fixed ideas about what he would and wouldn't wear in the garden – jeans, yes, but cords, no, plain jumpers in dark colours, yes, fleeces or anoraks, no. Out of the garden, he was equally firm in his sartorial views. It had to be a major, major occasion for him to wear a suit and tie – receiving an honorary MSc at his old college would just about qualify. In fact, he found it repugnant even to have a suit hanging in his wardrobe, so if a grand occasion arose (and he couldn't get out of it), Tony would get a call from him. 'Can I borrow the suit next week?' Not '*your* suit', you notice, but '*the* suit'. So trying to persuade him into fashionable clothes in the

garden was a non-starter, and he tried to persuade his fellow presenters to resist too. Nigel Colborn recalls Geoff saying in typically
blunt fashion, 'What were you dressed up as last week? You looked
like a Wardour Street pox doctor!'

But some of Geoff's disagreements with policy were more serious.
When the programme first adopted a magazine format, Geoff felt
that the practical, get-your-hands-dirty gardening had become side-
lined in favour of more frivolous items – a view he felt was strongly
supported by the fact that the pile of letters he used to receive each
week from viewers wanting information had slowed to a trickle, and
that the viewing figures were down. When Catalyst Television was
invited to take over, managing director Tony Laryea had a meeting
with Geoff very early on and assured him that he was the programme's greatest asset and that practical gardening would always be
at its core.

Later, in the mid-1990s, Geoff felt the programme had lost its way
again, this time by becoming, in his words, too up-market and
colour-supplement. Geoff used to say to the team, 'Come with me
to a garden centre one weekend and hear what our viewers really
want. They don't want art, they don't want grand gardens – what
they want is practical gardening.' 'And he was right,' says Tony
Laryea. 'He did know his audience extremely well.'

And his audience knew him extremely well too. Over the years
Geoff's fame had grown to such an extent that he could visit few
places in the world – even Goa – where he wasn't recognized by
someone usually wanting a gardening question answered. But neither
Geoff nor anyone close to him (except, perhaps, Tony) realized just
how famous he was, or how well loved, until after he died. Tony
knew because he was mistaken for Geoff everywhere he went. On
one occasion he was in a restaurant when a young lady approached
him, threw her arms round his neck and said, 'My hero! You're Geoff
Hamilton, aren't you?' Tony, of course, explained politely that he

wasn't. When he told Geoff about the incident he was curious to know what Tony had said. Tony, always alert to the need to keep his brother's feet firmly on the ground, replied, 'I said, "Yes, I am! Clear off!"' The look on Geoff's face was sufficient reward for the lie, and Tony felt he'd done his duty.

But one of Tony's most treasured memories is the day Geoff came back from filming in Glasgow, a big grin on his face. Sitting on the plane on the flight up, he heard two businessmen talking behind him. When the plane landed and he got up to leave, one of them grabbed his arm and said, 'Hey, don't I know you?' Geoff preened himself and got ready to accept their compliments with good grace when the man went on, 'Aren't you Tony Hamilton's brother?' They just happened to be clients of Tony's. It's the only time it ever happened, but Tony never let Geoff forget it.

Francesca Kay still finds people come into the medieval garden in an almost reverential way, wanting to see the place where Geoff had sat. 'They all want to know about him and ask me lots of questions. I must be the only person who met him for just one day who has to talk about him all the time.'

Geoff was always in great demand to appear at garden centres or to open fêtes, and, since his time was very limited, he used to do the former to make money and the latter for causes he believed in. Laurence Vulliamy, producer of *Gardeners' World* in the mid-1990s, recalls asking Geoff to open a fête in aid of a local charity near his home village in Oxfordshire. 'He agreed, though it was a round trip of 160 miles and meant giving up most of his Saturday. That afternoon, the heavens opened and it chucked it down, so only a few brave souls made it, but Geoff treated it as though it were a big occasion and made a very funny speech. "Ladies and gentlemen," he said, "I am honoured to be the filling in such a highly esteemed sandwich. Last year you had Dame Thora Hird, and next year you'll have Douglas Hurd, but this year I'll be lucky to be seen, let alone heard!" And he stayed in one of the tents for three hours afterwards answering people's questions.'

Whenever Geoff appeared in public, at garden centres or at *Gardeners' World Live*, there would always be a huge crush of people around him. Paula McWaters will never forget the time when Geoff was booked to do two talks at the *Country Living* Fair in London. The magazine had decided the fairest way to distribute the tickets for Geoff's talks was to give them out as people arrived. The tickets for the first talk had gone within ten minutes of the doors opening, so people asked if they could have tickets for the second talk in the afternoon. But the staff explained that as the tickets for the fair itself were timed, it would be unjust to the second wave of ticket-holders if all the seats for Geoff's afternoon talk had gone before they arrived. They saw the logic of that, but asked where they could start queuing up for the afternoon tickets. This was at about 10.10 a.m. and they were prepared to queue for nearly three hours. Just after 1 o'clock there were two enormous queues for the second talk, and again all the tickets were gone within minutes. 'I have never known anything like it. There were people puce in the face with anger, people in tears. I had one woman clutching my arm and saying, "But you don't understand. I've come all the way from Plymouth and I've only come to see Geoff. You must let me in!" I explained that fire regulations meant we would be breaking the law if we let even one more person in, but it didn't make any difference. In the end Geoff came to our rescue and agreed to give an extra talk.'

Geoff always fiercely fended off any suggestions that he was a star, and certainly chose not to become a TV personality. He was happy to appear with Ruby Wax or Lenny Henry for *Comic Relief*, or take part in a very funny sketch for *Children in Need* with Lionel Blair pretending to do all the close-ups because Geoff was too big a star actually to get his hands dirty, because the programmes were for charity. While he did a few shows like *Call My Bluff* and *A Good*

Read on Radio 4, he decided it wasn't for him. He was a gardener, not a celebrity.

Geoff's attitude to his fame was ambivalent. He used to say to Tony, 'When I die I believe it will be an entirely insignificant event.' 'Quite wrong, of course,' says Tony, 'but it does give an insight into his view of his success.' Andrew Gosling, who produced and directed *Cottage Gardens*, believes that fame was important to him because it gave him a sense of security and endorsed his views.

Stephen, his eldest son, feels he also enjoyed the fact that fame gave him direct access to other gardeners, who related to him very easily because they felt he was an ordinary gardener like them, but he just happened to be on television. 'He loved knocking ideas backwards and forwards with other gardeners, hearing how they did things, and fame gave him an ideal opportunity to do that wherever he went.'

Geoff was also aware of the power that it gave him – as Nick says, had he told the gardeners of Britain to take a chain saw to their ley-landii hedges, they would have done it – but he used his position responsibly to put across the things he believed in. While people in the garden chemicals and peat industry were unhappy because Geoff never used their products on screen or off it, he would have argued that he was simply showing viewers how he gardened, very success-fully without the need for chemicals or peat.

He wouldn't have been human if he hadn't enjoyed people telling him how much they liked what he did. John Kenyon remembers that when they were on the road filming they would often end the evening in a hotel bar. 'I noticed that whenever people came up and said how much they liked the programme, Geoff would chat to them quite happily. If they said, "What the hell were you playing at last week?" he would turn to me and say, "May I introduce John Kenyon, the producer."'

But he certainly didn't believe his own publicity, and used to relish the few vitriolic letters that came his way to the extent of pinning them on the wall in the downstairs loo at Barnsdale, the one that all the visitors used. 'Dear sir,' wrote one irate viewer, 'I wish you would encourage Geoff Hamilton to concentrate on what he is supposed to do – telling us about the garden concerned instead of wasting the short 25 minutes with his inane chatter. I class him as a pompous prattler.'

Another viewer was also irritated, but for different reasons. 'Well now folks, don't get me wrong. Geoff Hamilton has an interesting style. HE SOUNDS LIKE A SALOON BAR KNOW-IT-ALL, ALL MATEY ONE MINUTE AND THEN ALL BLUSTERY THE NEXT. But I don't know why he puts some sentences into capitals and some in heavy type. AND NO ONE WOULD DESCRIBE HIM AS AN OUTSTAND-ING WRITER OR THINKER. IS GEOFF ONLY PRETENDING TO BE ONE OF THE LADS? IS HE REALLY A MEMBER OF THE LANDED GENTRY? Let's face it, chums, he seems to live like a lord. What's the secret, Geoffo?'

He pinned up these letters, he said, as a constant reminder that not everyone liked him. 'Most people say such nice things that it's easy to think you're someone special. As soon as you think that, you lose it all.' He also enjoyed beng gently sent up by the likes of the *Guardian*'s TV critic Nancy Banks-Smith, who was a great fan of Geoff's. One piece of hers began, 'The question which agitates the nation today is what are we going to do about Geoff Hamilton's trousers? I would describe them as organic. The trousers have a battle-hardened air, like a soldier returning from the Hundred Years War. They are deeply furrowed at the top as if in thought, and the knees surprisingly seem to be half-way down the calf. Either Mr Hamilton has very amusing legs or the trousers have a life of their own and can, at a pinch, muck out the marrows on their own.'

While he was usually happy to talk to gardeners one to one and answer their questions, he didn't enjoy being surrounded by crowds of people, and he wanted to be able to have a private life with Lynda – one reason they usually went to the same few local restaurants where everyone knew them, so nobody bothered them.

Being a celebrity had its downside sometimes, though. When Chris was a student, his registered address was Barnsdale, so his unemployment cheque had to be cashed at the local post office, which could prove difficult when he was looking for work elsewhere. Once, he sent the cheque, endorsed on the back to Geoff, and asked him to cash it. Geoff was very reluctant to be seen in the local post office cashing a dole cheque, but eventually he went in and said to the attractive young woman behind the counter, 'I wouldn't like people to think I was drawing the dole. It's for my son, you know.' 'I wouldn't worry, Mr Hamilton,' she said. 'I expect they think you're drawing your pension!'

On other occasions, a famous face proved to be very useful. To the end of his life, Geoff refused to have a credit card or even a cheque guarantee card, preferring where possible to pay cash. One day he happened to be in London for a press conference and found himself in Hatchards bookshop in Piccadilly. He decided to treat himself to a very expensive set of horticultural reference books for which he didn't have enough cash, so he pulled out his cheque book. 'Do you have any identification, sir?' the assistant asked. Geoff stretched across and picked from a nearby shelf a copy of his *Gardeners' World Practical Gardening Course* with his photograph prominently on the front cover. 'Will this do?' he asked.

Gardeners' World ran from early spring to early autumn, so in the intervening months there was room in the schedules for other six-part gardening series, like *Geoffrey Smith's World of Flowers*, *The Victorian Kitchen Garden* and so on.

In 1985 Geoff did a couple of series about houseplants, called *Going to Pot*. His co-presenter was Susan Hampshire. 'Geoff was very, very good to work with,' she recalls. 'It was wonderfully reassuring to have someone so knowledgeable there. He virtually wrote everything for me, and I just voiced it, as it were. We got on very well because he knew that I genuinely loved plants and gardens and gardening. I'm afraid we did get the giggles quite often, and all in all it was a very pleasurable experience.'

Late in 1987 I had a phone call from Geoff. I was a freelance journalist then, writing about a range of topics, but I had got to know Geoff quite well at various gardening press receptions I went to in my capacity as gardening columnist for *Woman* magazine. He said the BBC was planning a gardening series called *First Time Garden*, with Denis Gartside producing. It aimed to show how to make a garden out of the mud heap the builders leave you with when you buy a brand-new house. They needed a female presenter, and he had suggested me. Was I interested? Was I!

'I find it's always best with Denis,' Geoff said, 'if he thinks things are his idea, so when he rings you, don't mention that we've had this conversation!' When Denis did ring a few days later I didn't mention the conversation I'd had with Geoff, and I got the job.

We started work in February 1988 in a small back garden near Cadbury's factory in Bournville, backing on to the main Birmingham to Bristol railway line. The garden was small and typical of a first-timer's plot – a few inches of topsoil skimmed over heavy clay subsoil and almost two skips full of breeze blocks, broken bricks, reels of wire and so on. It was bitterly cold and very wet, with thick ankle-deep mud. Geoff wasn't at all happy about working in those conditions, not because it was very unpleasant for us but because it was bad practice and the last thing we ought to have been showing new gardeners. But we had to get on because of the filming schedule, so we worked precariously from scaffolding boards laid across the mud. He was very supportive, very free with advice when asked, but very careful not to make me feel the raw beginner I was. If I got something wrong, he would discreetly put me right.

Geoff worked incredibly hard, and not just when the cameras were rolling. We were showing how to put up a fence, and while we needed to film only the first couple of panels going up, we also needed to show how to cut a fence panel to fit at the far end. So Geoff put up all the intervening panels himself with no cameras rolling so that we could show the final half-panel going in.

To have the garden ready for the next stage of filming each week, a firm of contractors was hired. But since they were not used to working to television deadlines, we would sometimes arrive at the garden to find that it wasn't ready. One day when we were scheduled to start planting, we arrived to find that the borders had not been dug over as expected. Instead, a few inches of topsoil had been spread across the heavy clay. Having been used to working at Barnsdale, where he made sure that everything was always ready for filming, Geoff found it all very frustrating. He immediately picked up a spade, started to dig, and injured his back – an injury that had him lying flat for a week.

Geoff wrote the book that accompanied the series. He had written several *Gardeners' World* books or booklets for the BBC, and they had all done well. He enjoyed writing and was very disciplined, always setting aside time every day – usually between 8 and 10 in the evening – to get on with it.

He wrote over 20 books, and Billy Ivory, the screenwriter responsible for BBC1's *Common as Muck*, who is Tony's son-in-law, is full of admiration. 'After Geoff died, I worked in his office for a while, and there on a shelf were all his books. To have sustained that level of creative energy for so many years is such an achievement. He had a rubbish bin, on the side of which he'd written, "The art of creative gardening starts here". It was a genuinely inspiring place to work. I'd been trying to finish a series for six years, and I did finish it in Geoff's office.'

Since the books had to be started before the series, it usually meant that, by the time filming began, Geoff had done most of the research and had a very clear idea of what the content of the series should be. And although the final editorial control always rested with the producer, all those who worked with Geoff were smart enough to realize that he knew far more about gardening than anyone else on the shoot, and so it was always a collaboration.

The follow-up series we did in 1989, *First Time Planting*, was made, not surprisingly, at Barnsdale in a small fenced-off area of the garden. The idea was to show new gardeners how to choose the right plants for the conditions in their gardens by planting up four different borders – facing north, east, south and west respectively – each of which required different types of plants. Since I wrote the accompanying book with Geoff as consultant, I suggested planting plans for the four borders for Geoff's approval. There was a slight hiccup when it came to planting the west-facing border. We had agreed on a theme – scented plants and pastel colours, since it would catch the late sun and was therefore an attractive place to sit in the evening. The plants that had been assembled for planting, though, included a wine-red berberis with orange flowers and a bright gold conifer, which were neither pastel nor scented. But one of the joys of working at Barnsdale was that finding substitutes was relatively easy, so we were able to rustle up something much more suitable.

During the filming I was between five and eight months pregnant with my second son, who remained hidden under a large, baggy and extremely hot jumper. Geoff and I did discuss whether we should refer to my pregnancy in the programme or not – 'Well, Gay, it looks as though you've been doing a little propagating of your own, ho, ho ho!' – and in the end decided not to. There does exist a photograph of Geoff and me stomach to stomach, with mine only slightly larger and, what's more, as I gleefully pointed out to him, only temporary!

While we were filming that series in the summer of 1989, another garden was being built at Barnsdale – the Ornamental Kitchen

Garden. Here Geoff wanted to show that while most small gardens can't sustain a separate vegetable plot, there is no reason why some crops can't be grown in among the flower borders. Besides, many vegetables are striking plants which will enhance the beauty of the border. Growing them among other plants also makes them less likely to suffer from pests and diseases, since they are neither *en masse* nor exposed in open rows.

Originally, the OK Garden, as it was known, was built in 1990 as the feature garden for *Gardeners' World*, since Geoff always created a new garden for the programme every year. But that year Mark Kershaw and John Kenyon managed to persuade the BBC that it would make a good separate six-part series. BBC Books also felt it would make an interesting book, so Geoff started work doing extensive research by reading historical texts and talking to a wide range of specialists, both scientists and experienced cottage gardeners who had worked this way all their lives.

'We had a marvellous opportunity to show how a garden develops,' says Mark Kershaw. 'We already had the first OK Garden, which by the time we started making the series was a year old, so we built an identical one next door to it so that we could show how it had been constructed and planted, in stages, as the series progressed. By the time the series had been shot and was being edited, the first garden had had another season's growth, so we were able to show three years' development.' It was the first gardening series to move backwards and forwards in time, and Mark Kershaw wanted to let the viewers know right from the start what was happening so there wouldn't be any confusion. It involved very careful planning, with Mark having to know a year ahead in some instances exactly what he was going to be shooting and how it would all fit together.

In one sequence, for the programme called 'Somewhere to Sit', he wanted Geoff to do his opening piece setting out the theme and

Geoff in his favourite part of Barnsdale, the woodland garden, with the 'khasi' – the hermitage he built for *Paradise Gardens* – in the background.

No longer two peas in a pod. Even without the glasses, it's not difficult to tell Geoff and Tony apart.

One Moss Geoff was always happy to see on his lawn. This is one of Lynda's favourite pictures.

Son Stephen, who recorded Geoff's gardening life with his camera.

Geoff with Lynda and her two sons Jeremy and William.

Mowing Versailles. Geoff got great pleasure from even the most routine of gardening jobs.

A rare sighting of Geoff in a suit and tie, receiving his honorary M.Sc. from HRH the Duchess of Kent at Writtle College. Professor Mike Salmon delivered the citation.

One of the few occasions Geoff went in for giant vegetable growing.

The Country Garden had everything Geoff thought a 'paradise garden' should have – water, a profusion of plants and somewhere to sit and contemplate.

Professor David Bellamy, in June 1997, dedicating the Winskill Stones to Geoff's memory after their purchase by Plantlife.

The opening of Seaton Meadows near Barnsdale in June 1997 with five Hamiltons present: (left to right) Carol, Lynda, Tony, Pippa Greenwood, Adrian Darby, chairman of Plantlife, Nick and Chris.

Living memorials to Geoff – *Rosa* 'Geoff Hamilton', a new English rose bred by David Austin, and *Penstemon* 'Geoff Hamilton', bred by Clive and Kathy Gandley.

Joie de vivre – Geoff in jocular mood cycling down the drive at Barnsdale at snowdrop time.

then start to crouch as if he were about to sit down, although there was no seat beneath him, just bare earth. Geoff didn't understand what Mark was up to, but trusted him and did as he was asked. A year later, Mark finished the sequence with Geoff settling down on to a real seat underneath a pergola in exactly the same spot. The camera had been in precisely the same place both times, so that when the sequence was cut together, the seat and pergola appeared as if by magic behind him just as Geoff started to sit down. 'He was really chuffed with that,' Mark recalls, 'and used to tell people about it all the time.'

The Ornamental Kitchen Garden was one of Geoff's favourite series and the garden carried on appearing in *Gardeners' World* right up until the time of his death.

With the production traumas of *First Time Garden* healed, in 1991 Geoff was persuaded to venture out into real gardens once more for the third series we did together, *Old Garden, New Gardener*, again aimed at beginners. It was done in three real gardens in Rugby, which were typical of those a novice gardener might have to tackle – an over-mature garden, a boring garden and a narrow rubbish-filled city yard. One sequence featured the problem of what to do with overgrown leylandii hedges. To make the shot dramatic, Geoff was filmed against a hedge describing the problem, and then the camera pulled back to reveal he was standing in the basket of a 'cherry picker' some 15 feet (4.5 m) above the ground. It was something that took courage on his part since Geoff really didn't like heights.

By this time Geoff had become extremely interested in environmental issues and how they related to gardeners (see Chapter 7). His next series, made in 1992, was *The Living Garden*, in which he set out to show how working with nature and understanding the natural ecology of a garden can make you a better and more successful gardener. One of the most enduring images of that series is of Geoff in the middle of a vast field of cabbages, making the point that growing one crop on this kind of scale was an invitation to every pest for miles around. As the camera, on top of a very high crane, pulls out, it reveals thousands of cabbages, and among them, spelt out in white, are the words EAT AT JOE'S. 'It was Geoff's idea,' said the series producer, Mick Rhodes, 'and it took some organizing. First there was getting a 132-foot- (40-m)-high crane in position, getting police permission to block the road in the process, and working out exactly where Geoff and the words had to be if they were to be within the camera's field of vision. The words were made from cabbages cut in half to reveal the white centre, so there were all the cabbages to be cut. That hard, cold, wet work was done by Carrie Tooth, the heroic production manager, with a team of local people. It wasn't until I finally got up on the crane and looked through the camera that I realized the words weren't clear enough, so we had to use all the halves we'd sliced off, the wrong way up, to fill in the gaps. It was a bitterly cold February day, so we were beginning to lose the light by mid-afternoon and we'd heard that there was a storm with strong winds heading our way. By the time everything was ready, we had only one real chance to get it right and, of course, Geoff did it perfectly first time.'

Geoff never ceased to amaze Tony with the ideas he had for television series. His next theme was cottage gardens, because he felt strongly that that style of planting was one of the most relevant for the small gardens most people have these days. His publishers, BBC Books, thought it was an excellent idea, and so commissioned a book (they were right: it sold over 250,000 copies). But the system for commissioning television series within the BBC is somewhat more complicated and Geoff didn't know for some time whether there would be a six-part series. In 1993 he decided to start work on building the two gardens, the Artisan's Garden and the Gentleman's Garden, at Barnsdale anyway, and if the series didn't happen, they would be the feature gardens for *Gardeners' World* the following year.

But the six-part series was commissioned in 1994. The producer was Andrew Gosling, a very experienced and award-winning documentary film-maker who had worked with Geoff since 1991 on *Gardeners' World*, so he already knew what an exceptionally good presenter Geoff was. Although people often say about Geoff that what you saw was what you got, Andrew believes it wasn't that simple. 'Geoff was a natural showman, and he realized that if you are just yourself on camera you don't come across. So what you saw was a contruct based very closely on Geoff Hamilton. He had decided who he was and what bits of himself he wanted to present to the camera, and that's what he did brilliantly.'

By the time Andrew started work on *Cottage Gardens*, the two gardens had been started, and research for the book was well under way. 'I said to Geoff early on, "I'm not entirely sure what a cottage garden is," and he said, "Nor am I. I think it can be anything that you want it to be!"' While Geoff was doing the research for his book, he borrowed from me a book on the history of cottage gardens that was out of print. I teased him, reminding him of the advice in the old Tom Lehrer song to 'plagiarize, plagiarize. Let no one else's work evade your eyes.' He laughed and said, 'If you only read one book, it's plagiarism, but if you read two it's called research!'

In addition to the gardens being built at Barnsdale, the team visited cottage gardens all over the country. Undoubtedly, one of the cottage gardeners who made the most lasting impression on the audience, and on Geoff, was Great-Uncle George Flatt, the retired farm worker from East Anglia. He was the great-uncle of someone Andrew's parents knew and was such an amazing character that, even though Andrew couldn't see his garden at all on the day he went to visit because it was under several feet of snow, he decided they must include him in the series even if his garden was awful.

Geoff didn't meet him until the day of filming and was completely captivated by him. 'He represented everything Geoff felt gardening should be about – all the things closest to his heart – and none of the things he didn't like, such as heavy over-design. Geoff said afterwards, "He does everything wrong, yet it works!" There was a political edge there, too, for Geoff, because Great-Uncle George had been a farm worker, working incredibly long hours for very little money, to whom his garden was a vital resource, to feed the family.'

The unit was small – Sarah Greene, the production manager (nicknamed 'Robert Post's child' by Geoff after Flora Post, the heroine of Stella Gibbons's famous satire on rural life, *Cold Comfort Farm*), cameraman John Couzens, sound recordist John Gilbert, Andrew and Geoff. They spent a lot of time on the road together, so that they quickly became like family. 'Sarah got married during the making of the series, so Geoff and I gave her a stag night,' Andrew said. 'Given both our track records in the marriage department, we drank a toast in champagne to her *first* wedding!'

The series, transmitted in January 1995, was a huge success, with audiences of over five million viewers per episode, the highest figure for any gardening series. The figures went up as the series went on – word spread rapidly, with people telling their friends to watch.

Geoff had already started thinking about the next series, provisionally called *Geoff Hamilton's Country Retreats*, for which he would build the two gardens and start filming during the summer of 1995 and complete it in 1996 for transmission in January 1997.

But in a sense Geoff was the victim of his own success. Keen to follow up the great success of *Geoff Hamilton's Cottage Gardens* sooner rather than later, the BBC put pressure on Geoff to bring the series forward a year, to film the whole thing from start to finish that summer ready for transmission in January 1996. That would have meant that instead of there being a whole year for the gardens he built to grow, as there had been for the two cottage gardens, there would be at most four months since the gardens hadn't even been started at that point. Geoff was very concerned because the plants simply wouldn't be mature, and the gardens would not reach his high standard, but, reluctant to let the side down, he agreed.

The theme of the series, that was finally to be called *Geoff Hamilton's Paradise Gardens*, was set out very clearly by him in the introduction to the accompanying book. 'I am convinced that we all need some kind of escape from the complexity, the pressure and the ever-accelerating speed of modern life, a life just about as far removed from the one for which our minds and bodies were originally designed as it's possible to get. I'm certain, too, that most of us are desperate for a philosophy that counters our current passion for materialism and the shallow values of "sophisticated society". I firmly believe that the garden presents us with a controlled situation where we can have the best of the rural existence without any of the drawbacks.'

They started filming in June, and on the first day they shot an interview with the owner of an extraordinary roof garden in Chelsea. Since Geoff was in London, somewhere he thoroughly disliked and didn't visit unless strictly necessary, the producer of the series, Ray Hough, a very experienced documentary film-maker, decided to make use of the opportunity to shoot the opening sequence. 'Since the theme of the series was escaping from the stresses of modern living, I thought where better to show exactly what he was talking about than by the side of the A40 at White City in London during the afternoon rush hour, so that's where he stood to record his opening piece to camera. We were right by the big White City estate, and I think he was genuinely shocked by what he saw. "People shouldn't have to live like this," he kept saying. And that's where we got the idea that we had to show that even in a block of flats like that, you could still grow plants, and so bring the countryside into your life to provide the relaxation you need.'

The next day's filming was in the Country Garden built for the series at Barnsdale. The night before, when they had all met up at the hotel where the team was staying, Geoff had seemed uncharacteristically anxious about things. 'He was worrying because he felt that some of the material wasn't in the right order. This wasn't a problem at all because we had only just started shooting, and anyway, with a series like this, the final order is only really decided when it's all shot and is in the process of being edited.'

The next morning Geoff seemed fine, doing the sort of job he enjoyed most, laying the patio in the Country Garden from an assortment of old bricks, slabs, paviours, tiles and even terracotta pipes. After lunch, though, he said he didn't feel well and eventually was persuaded to go up to the house and lie down. The next thing the team heard was the siren of an ambulance. Geoff had had a heart attack and was taken to the Leicester Royal Infirmary. It was on the television news and in the papers, and thousands of get-well cards and letters began pouring in.

Geoff had been due to be at *Gardeners' World Live* at the National Exhibition Centre in Birmingham the following week, so Alan Titchmarsh stepped into the breach, and he and I presented the *Gardeners' World* coverage of the show. It's always difficult to move around the show because of the crowds, but it was even more difficult that year because everywhere we went exhibitors, journalists and members of the public were stopping us to ask how Geoff was and to send him their best wishes for a speedy recovery.

Fortunately, it was only a mild heart attack and within a few days the doctors felt able to move him out of intensive care – or to pot him on, as one of them rather wittily put it. Within a week he was allowed home, with strict instructions not to work for eight weeks, and he was put on a course of beta-blockers. On them, Stephen recalls, he was a very different man. 'He was so much more laid back than he'd ever been. When we shot the cover of the *Paradise Gardens* book, we had to wait for about two hours for the light to be right and instead of the usual "Come on! Come on! Get on with it!" he was happy just to sit and chat, and it was terrific. But I don't think he liked being like that because it was the intensity, the nervous energy that made him the man he was.'

In the meantime, with the series postponed until January 1997, the *Paradise Gardens* team carried on as best they could without Geoff, researching and doing a few interviews that couldn't wait. Eight weeks later he was back. 'He was completely back to normal,' Ray Hough recalls, 'full of life, full of vigour, eager to crack on and not stressed at all – just like the man I'd seen on the telly. He was striding through the gardens, so that we all had a job to keep up with him, and he certainly seemed the fittest of all of us.'

Over the next year, Geoff loved making the series. He thoroughly enjoyed his day spent with Horace and Millie Hunt in their garden in Oxfordshire. They had never had much money, but their sheer contentment with their lot and their pleasure in their garden was exactly what Geoff thought the series was about. He enjoyed his day in the medieval garden with Francesca Kay, but most of all he loved building and planting the gardens at Barnsdale. One of his favourite ventures was a hermitage in the woods. It was a tiny thatched hut, which resembled the hermitages the Victorians used to build to house a real hermit – so that he could be shown off to their friends. He loved it, but the crew christened it 'the khasi' and Ray Hough threatened to put the sound of a lavatory chain being pulled on to the soundtrack. In the end the hermitage never appeared in the series, but it provided a lot of ribald jokes and laughter.

Some of the sequences involved a process called blue screen, where the presenter is filming against a background of a particular shade of blue, on which all sorts of moving images can be imposed afterwards – in this case, low-flying aircraft, city streets and other urban images. Normally you use cloth, but outside in a garden it can be very hard to keep it still, so Geoff said, 'I don't know what you're up to, boy, but if you provide the paint, I'll knock up a hardboard screen.'

It was very windy the day they shot the scene, so there were four strong men, grunting and groaning as they struggled to hold the screen steady behind Geoff while he did a very emotive piece to camera.

Some other sequences were very complicated to shoot. There was one where Geoff had to name all the plants in his wheelbarrow, then walk past a line of plants, naming each one out of vision and then pop out in front of the camera again at the end. What with plane noise or the timing for the camera moves being slightly out, it took 16 takes to get it right, but Ray remembers that Geoff was as happy at the end of it as he had been at the beginning. 'If he felt it was worth doing and he knew we were all striving to do something special, he was endlessly patient.'

Even so, he was always concerned that *Paradise Gardens* wouldn't look as good as the *Cottage Gardens* series. 'In the last week of July,' Ray Hough recalls, 'after we'd done the last bits of filming in the gardens and Geoff had done his last piece to camera, as we were walking away, he turned to me and said, "We've pulled it off, boy. We're there!"'

By now Geoff was as busy as ever. He had decided that he didn't like the way the beta-blockers slowed him down, and so he had gradually weaned himself off them. During that summer he had taken a major decision. After 16 years on *Gardeners' World*, he had decided that he'd had enough. The BBC had offered him his own series, *Geoff Hamilton's Gardening Week*, on BBC1. His one burning ambition was to see gardening on BBC1, so it was an offer he couldn't refuse. It would be just Geoff and some guests at Barnsdale doing what he liked doing most – down-to-earth, practical gardening. Although it was to go out in daytime to start with, the suggestion was made that if it were a huge success it might move to an early-evening slot on BBC1, with its potentially larger audiences, a challenge that Geoff relished.

The plan was that he would do the new series beginning in late September and running through to Christmas. In 1997 he would start the new series of *Gardeners' World*, and then at Easter hand over to Alan Titchmarsh to whom Geoff was delighted to pass the programme. Then he'd start the second series of *Geoff Hamilton's Gardening Week*.

He spent the Friday in the garden, filming the opening title sequence for the new series, full of enthusiasm and energy. On the Sunday he had his second, fatal heart attack.

Geoff Hamilton's Paradise Gardens was finished that autumn, with Tony Hamilton speaking the commentary that Geoff had never got round to recording. For Tony, even though he was aware that he could never match Geoff's professionalism, it was an enormous privilege to help to finish something his brother had made so well. For Ray Hough it was the most difficult thing he had ever done. 'I really felt I was making the series for one man, and what was so hard at the end was never knowing whether he would have thought it was all right. And also, when we were editing, there he was all day, every day, on the screen, so full of life that it wasn't until we'd finally finished that it sank in that he had gone.'

Geoff would have been amused and pleased to know that the man who started working with him knowing nothing about gardening at all, and having no interest in it, has become, like so many other people, a very keen gardener purely because of him.

The series went out early in 1997 and won the hearts of its millions of viewers. It showed a deeper, more reflective, even spiritual side of Geoff and felt closer to his heart than anything he had done before. It was a fitting tribute to a complex, kind and dedicated man.

CHAPTER SEVEN

THE GREEN MAN

From his earliest childhood Geoff was interested in the natural world. He not only enjoyed growing plants from very early on but he also loved being out in the countryside, camping with the Scouts, or walking in the woods with Tony, building shelters to sleep in, living off the land, summer and winter and in all weathers. Of course, no one used terms like 'environment' when Geoff was a boy, a period of few cars, very little new building and still so much untouched land that no one perceived that there was any threat to it.

In the early 1950s, when Geoff's gardening career got under way, almost everyone who gardened used peat for conditioning soil and potting, and almost everyone used chemical fertilizers and pesticides without a second thought. Geoff did too. In the *Gardeners' World Vegetable Book*, which he wrote in 1981, he recommends a range of chemicals for controlling weeds and pests, though he did try some non-chemical methods of control. He described one experiment he did to ward off cabbage root fly: 'The first three rows were treated with proprietory soil insecticides. I used diazinon, chlorpyriphos and bromophos. The fourth and fifth rows were devoted to old gardeners' remedies. In one I put a piece of rhubarb in the planting hole, and the other a couple of mothballs. The plants in the next row were protected physically by placing a bit of foam rubber round the stem. The last two rows were untreated, as a control... The two untreated rows went down like ninepins. The two rows treated with mothballs and rhubarb also, I'm afraid, succumbed to attack. All three chemically treated rows escaped, with the exception of one plant treated with bromophos. The physical barrier of foam rubber also gave complete control and is therefore an excellent method, particularly if you would prefer to use chemicals only as a last resort.'

Geoff also used peat in those days, seeing it as preferable to loam-based composts for sowing vegetables. 'Good loam is getting more and more difficult to come by, yet there still seems to be a plentiful supply of peat. Apart from the obvious advantages of availability, peat composts have many points in their favour. They are light and easy to handle, they can be varied at will to suit a wide range of plants and they vary in quality far less than their soil-based counterparts. This means that they will produce exactly the same results time after time.'

Early in his BBC TV career Geoff went to the west coast of Ireland to visit a garden for *Gardeners' World* and, according to Lynda, it turned out to be something of a road to Damascus for him. 'He just hadn't realized what was happening before that. He chanced upon a man with a donkey and cart, just cutting a little bit of peat for his fire, and then beside him a huge commercial peat cutter ripping it out of the land. That, of course, was what was doing the damage.' He was horrified to think that the requirements of gardeners were destroying huge expanses of the countryside and with it the habitats of multitudes of animals and plants. He felt sure that most people just didn't know that, and that if they did, they'd try to find alternatives to peat.

Certainly, that's what *he* did. As soon as he realized that important natural habitats were being destroyed by the extraction of peat, Geoff decided to stop using it at Barnsdale altogether, just as soon as he could find a suitable substitute. Carol remembers Geoff finding out about coir. 'He did an awful lot of trials with coir, and spoke to everybody who knew anything about it. For a short time we were using both peat and coir, but then eventually Geoff became convinced about coir and thought it was the right way to go. Once he'd made a decision, having assembled all the facts, then that was that – you couldn't change his mind, so we didn't use anything but coir after that.'

In the early 1990s a government Commission of Enquiry looked into the whole issue of peat and the environment, and a relatively new, small charity called Plantlife, whose function was to campaign for the preservation of the habitats of wild plants, approached Geoff for help in preparing its submission to the commission. 'We needed a high-profile, environmentally aware media gardener,' says Plantlife's director, Dr Jane Smart, 'and when Geoff agreed to help us we couldn't believe our luck. He helped us in a number of ways, not least by being able to say that he was growing plants very successfully in coir. And what's more, he was prepared to show on television that it was possible to do it without peat. It is very hard to find high-profile media people who would go out on a limb for an issue, but Geoff was a brave man, and he appeared to be totally dedicated to his cause. I also think he had brilliant instincts for what his viewers wanted. He sensed that while he might upset a few people in the trade, his viewers would feel it was right that he got involved in something like this. What Geoff liked about the peat campaign, I think, was that instead of just offering doom and gloom about destroying the planet, he could offer gardeners a real solution to a big problem, and he really liked the fact that the ordinary gardener could do something to help save the world.'

In 1992 Geoff made a trip to Sri Lanka for *Gardeners' World* to see how coconut fibre was processed into coir. He felt it was a good use of a natural resource that would otherwise go to waste and also earned valuable foreign currency for a third-world country, as well as providing employment for people who would otherwise have no work.

As Geoff would have been the first to admit, coir isn't easy to use, and the mistake many people made was to try to treat it just like peat. So he often demonstrated on *Gardeners' World* how it should be used properly.

Geoff was so convinced that coir was viable that he not only used it in the programme but also used it exclusively at Barnsdale Plants. All the plants raised for sale were grown in coir – indeed, they still are – and if he hadn't been able to prove that it was possible to produce first-class plants in that way, it would have made no sense for Geoff, as a businessman, to persevere with it.

Geoff's conversion to coir did not go down well with the peat industry, and the BBC received complaints in 1991 on the grounds that programmes were meant to be impartial and the BBC was allowing Geoff to promote coir to the detriment of peat. The BBC took the view that Geoff was expressing an opinion to which he was entitled, and since coir wasn't a product manufactured by one company he wasn't in breach of any guidelines. In the spirit of fair play, though, *Gardeners' World* presented an item about peat in which Geoff put the case against the use of peat, while Peter Seabrook argued in favour. 'I felt that the peat industry wasn't getting a fair hearing, so I endeavoured to put their point of view,' Peter Seabrook says. 'After that, it was something about which Geoff and I agreed to differ.'

Adam Pasco, editor of *Gardeners' World* magazine, also used to get complaints from the industry about Geoff's position on peat and chemicals. 'I would always say that Geoff was entitled to his views and they weren't simply based on whim. They were based on extensive research. And also he showed clearly what he was talking about, so you could see for yourself whether it worked or not.'

The first time Geoff met Gordon Rae, now Director-General of the Royal Horticultural Society, at a press lunch in London, Gordon was working for ICI's Agrochemicals Division. 'Geoff made it clear very quickly that he was not in favour of the use of chemicals or peat. A robust exchange took place, which continued throughout lunch. At the end of lunch, we both agreed that gardening and horticulture were not just about pesticides and peat and there were many other areas we could agree on to the benefit of everyone.'

It was in the early 1980s that Geoff began to move away from using chemicals in the garden and started to become organic. In 1982 he established an organic garden at the old Barnsdale and, in 1983, began a trial in the vegetable garden comparing the success of organic methods with more conventional, chemical-based methods. The early trials were pretty disastrous, John Kenyon recalls, because, as Geoff learnt, it takes time − often several years − to succeed with organic gardening. Where no organic matter has been added to the soil for some years, it takes a while to get it back into good heart. It also takes a year or two for a garden to find its own natural balance in terms of pests and predators. You can't simply use organic products for a few months and then compare results with non-organic methods. But as time went on, Geoff became more and more committed to the whole idea, and better at it. 'I used to question him very hard indeed on some of the things he was doing,' John Kenyon says, 'because I felt that having someone on the programme not using any chemicals and not using peat-based composts might not necessarily be in the best interests of the viewers. So he had to convince me every time that what he was doing was sound.'

Although up until the late 1980s Geoff still did trials in the vegetable plot at Barnsdale comparing organic with inorganic methods, the main gardens were never sprayed with pesticides and nothing but organic fertilizers were ever used. To prove his point, Geoff compared the soil from the adjoining farmer's field, which had been fed with only chemical fertilizers, with the soil at Barnsdale, into which 100 tons of organic matter a year had been worked. The former was pale, hard and lumpy, difficult to break down and without a worm to be seen, while Barnsdale's soil was fine and crumbly, dark in colour and with half a dozen worms or more to every spadeful.

Geoff's influence on people's attitude to organic gardening was enormous because he made it seem perfectly normal, and showed that you didn't need to wear sandals or knit your own muesli to practise it. The paradox was that, until chemicals were invented, it had been the way everyone gardened, yet once garden chemicals were available, organic gardening was seen as fringe, alternative and a little eccentric.

As well as convincing large numbers of the British public that organic gardening was best, Geoff also convinced some of his colleagues. When Anne Swithinbank first started on *Gardeners' World*, she couldn't see the point of not spraying with selective insecticides that killed the pests but didn't harm the beneficial insects. 'Geoff always said, "No, leave well alone. Have faith – it will work if you leave it to sort itself out. Even if you spray with something that doesn't kill beneficial insects, you will drive the predators away because there's no food for them. When the chemical wears off and the pests return, there'll be nothing to eat them, so you'll have to use more chemicals." I do agree with him now, and I now garden more or less entirely organically.'

Pippa Greenwood, who started her career as a plant pathologist, always disagreed with Geoff about controlling greenfly, and he never managed to convince her. 'Geoff would use soft soap, which admittedly is "green", but it can also wipe out beneficial insects. I used to argue with him that it was better if you use a specific aphicide like pirimicarb that wouldn't harm the good guys, and I know he understood my logic. I think the answer is to have both solutions in your armoury and go for the green one first. I used to argue with him about blue tits, and greenfly too. He'd say, "The roses are covered in greenfly, but there's no need to spray because the blue tits will sort them out." I would say, "Come on, Geoff! Not everyone has blue tits in their garden and, besides, blue tits can't eat endless amounts of greenfly!"'

What Pippa liked about Geoff's attitude was that he never tried to make you feel guilty if you didn't share his views. What he did, she says, was just suggest that you looked at other ways of doing things. 'He never lectured, he just put his case and showed you the results.' To be fair, Geoff would often give a non-organic alternative on the programme – 'Give it some Growmore or rose fertilizer, or, if you're organic like me, use pelleted chicken manure.'

When head gardener Ian Spence first came to work at Barnsdale, he was a bit sceptical about organic gardening, though obviously he gardened the way Geoff wanted him to. 'But after eight years here, I am totally convinced that it is the way forward. Barnsdale is a testament to it. There was no spraying to get things looking good for the cameras. Once Geoff had made the decision not to use chemicals any more, that was it. He taught me to work with nature, not against it, and I will value the seven years I worked alongside Geoff for as long as I live.'

His brother Tony, too, has become a 100 per cent organic gardener since Geoff's death. If he dares even to take the sprayer out into his garden, he feels that a thunderbolt will strike him down. He well remembers how Geoff told him one day about an organic gardener he met in Yorkshire whose allotment had no sign of caterpillars or greenfly. When asked how he did it, he said, 'Ah do a lot o' lookin'.' He actually went around picking off the slugs and the other pests, and his garden was immaculate – with a lot of help from his natural friends. And this is now exactly what Tony does. Each evening, he and Carol have 'the tour', which means strolling round the garden 'doin' a lot o' lookin''. They feel Geoff would have approved of that.

While it mattered to Geoff that the produce he grew and ate was free from all chemicals, and that he could enjoy a myriad of butterflies and birds in his garden, his interest in organic gardening was increasingly part of his concern for the wider environment. He was disturbed by the effects on the countryside of agribusiness, with the wholesale destruction of hedgerows, and by monoculture on a vast scale, needing huge amounts of chemicals to control the pests it inevitably attracted. He was worried by the pollution caused by traffic and by the swaths of countryside disappearing under tarmac to service the ever-growing number of cars. He felt we had become cavalier about our environment because we had lost touch with nature. So many of us live in cities with little or no land around us, and all our food comes from supermarkets shrink-wrapped in plastic, so that many children grow up not knowing that vegetables grow in soil. And with crops like strawberries and lettuce available 52 weeks a year, we are losing touch with the seasons too.

In 1991 Geoff started work on *The Living Garden*, which was both a television series and a book. The text of the book was written in collaboration with Jennifer Owen, an experienced wildlife gardener, scientist and author. Geoff wrote the introduction himself, and in it he set out his philosophy very clearly. 'The garden is perhaps the one place left in our modern world,' he wrote, 'where we can get a practical "hands-on" experience of nature. As a species which is top of the natural heap, we can use our influence here to affect the millions of other plants and animals which share our space. It's up to us whether we use our powers in a benign or a malign way to benefit or to harass out of existence the living things in the lower orders.

'The choice is ours to engage in a war of wills with nature or to play the game by the natural rules. I believe that gardeners would prefer to live in peace and harmony with their fellow creatures and that the very essence of their pastime is to create a kind of natural Arcadia where all is sweetness and light. But, of course, the natural world simply isn't like that.

'We all know the chain of life depends on one species living off another. When the hawk is hungry its instinct is to kill the mouse and it does so without hesitation and certainly with no pangs of conscience. Likewise when the mouse needs to eat, it'll devour the complete seed crop of a particular plant with no thought for the survival of that particular species.

'Right up at our elevated end of the scale, our farmers will happily drench plants in poisonous sprays to kill every insect in sight in order that our species should survive. We'll kill weeds and wildflowers alike to reduce competition with food plants and, if that destroys the birds that feed on them, well so be it. After all, that's nature; it's a tough world out there and we must be ruthless in order to survive.

'The theory has perhaps worked well so far but now we're beginning to see ominous writing on the wall. It's started to dawn on us that we cannot simply live in isolation. Just as all levels of the natural order depend on a lower level for their existence, so do we. If we do poison them all out of existence, we simply destroy the very source of our lives.

'The one great proviso of our inheritance has always been that with power comes responsibility. Certainly we hold the destiny of every other species in our hands, but if we destroy them we destroy ourselves in the process.

'Well, there are bright signs on the horizon. With the realization of our dangerous position, scientific thinking is now seeking other ways of protecting food plants from pests and diseases, without actually killing them, and researching alternatives to polluting chemical fertilizers.

'It'll be a long and exacting process, but we gardeners have no need to wait. With none of the problems of the food producer – mono-culture and macroeconomics in particular – we can welcome our natural friends into the garden and observe with delight the perfec-tion of the natural system.

'We can live by nature's own rules, interfering only where absolutely necessary – and our prime position entitles us to do that. The result will be a garden of overwhelming natural beauty that buzzes with wildlife and delights and fascinates us every single day of our lives.'

What Geoff set out to do in both the series and the book was to explain the ecology of a garden, to show how the various life cycles – of bacteria, of plants, of all kinds of creatures – from mealy bugs to moles – work, and how they interact with each other to produce a living garden. He believed that once people knew a bit more about how their garden worked, then they would understand the conse-quences of their actions more clearly and so would be better, more environmentally aware gardeners and perhaps more conscious of their place in the wider scheme of things.

In one sequence in the series Geoff went to visit a 500-year-old oak tree in Sherwood Forest which is now dying, but which has been micropropagated so that an exact replica of the tree, planted beside it, will eventually take its place. He pointed out that the new tree would still be living when he had been dead for 500 years. 'I don't know about you,' he said, 'but that makes me feel quite humble. It makes you realize that our species is only a tiny part of the whole natural world, and that nature is not our enemy to be fought against. It is part of us and we are part of it.'

In the last years of his life Geoff had become increasingly interested in the environment. Having been a lifelong Labour voter, he did vote for the Green party in the European Community Elections of 1994 at a time when their star was rising and there seemed a good chance that they might win some seats. But he also got involved in environmental issues himself. He became closely linked with the charity Plantlife and was always willing to help and lend his name to their work since he firmly believed that without plant life there was no life.

Jane Smart, the director of Plantlife, was very impressed at the amount of time Geoff gave them. 'At the beginning, when we were still very small, we felt we weren't making best use of Geoff, but then, since we were so small and new, we didn't have the opportunities to use him better. So we had a very small meeting, just Sir William Wilkinson, former chairman of the Nature Conservancy Council, a couple of staff and Geoff, who bothered to come all the way to London just to give us the benefit of his advice.'

They knew he was popular but weren't aware of quite how popular until he opened one of the meadows that Plantlife had managed to buy – the Davies meadow in Herefordshire. There had been a piece in one of the Sunday papers the weekend before, saying that Geoff would buy a pint afterwards in the local pub for the first five people to join Plantlife. Geoff's fans turned up in force, and the first five new members were signed up in no time. Plantlife tried to give Geoff the money for the beer, but he wouldn't take it. 'I said I'd buy them a pint, and I will!'

In 1996 Geoff became patron of Plantlife's appeal to raise money to save the Winskill Stones, an area of what is called limestone pavement and a unique habitat for very rare plants. He had first seen a limestone pavement some ten years earlier, when he had been filming in Carnforth, Lancashire, with Roy Lancaster, near Roy's boyhood home. 'I told Geoff that not far from where we'd been filming there was a limestone pavement called Hutton's Roof, with really interesting plants growing in the clints and grikes. "Like what?" he asked, so I mentioned ferns unique to that area, the baneberry (*Actaea spicata*) and a special moor grass called sesleria. So on the way back to the hotel, we went up there and wandered about combing the area looking for these special plants. We found some ferns and eventually the baneberry, though it was only in leaf, not in flower. It was a very special time. Geoff really enjoyed it, and I could tell he felt at home there. It was getting dark as we drove back through the lanes, and it was all he talked about that night. He never forgot that trip, I know, and I'm sure it was a factor in his passion to save the limestone pavement.'

Plantlife's campaign to save the Winskill Stones was launched in May 1996, and Geoff's name was also attached to the Lottery application for a £250,000 grant to achieve their goal. Again, he liked the fact that it was an issue that ordinary gardeners could do something about without a great deal of sacrifice on their part. Since it was mainly for rockery stone that the limestone pavements were being destroyed, gardeners could make a real difference very easily by simply not buying it any more. Although they could use other natural stone that was in plentiful supply, Geoff went one step further and suggested that people make their own rocks (see page 121).

Geoff tried to be as green as possible in his own life. He recycled wherever possible, and was anything but a conspicuous consumer. He bought books – serious modern fiction, like Robertson Davies and Anita Brookner, and classics, with Thomas Hardy and Scott Fitzgerald among his favourites – and records – jazz and classical – but that was about it.

He did have a Land Rover Discovery because living in the heart of the country as he did it wasn't possible to rely on public transport and, besides, he often needed the car to transport materials. Tony used to tease him about it and say that an old Mini would do just as well, but Geoff got a kick out of his car and felt he was entitled to at least one toy. Yet whenever he could travel by train he did, and he loved to cycle. He and Lynda used to enjoy cycling holidays in France, and after his first heart attack he took up cycling on a daily basis for the exercise.

Not surprisingly, he was approached in 1995 by another environ-mental charity – Sustrans, which stands for sustainable transport – which was setting up cycle paths all over the country with the goal of enabling people to cycle the length and breadth of the country on specially designated paths. Sybille Reisen from the Wales and south-west branch of the charity wrote and asked Geoff if he would take part in the 25-mile cycle ride they were planning in August from Brecon to Merthyr over the Brecon Beacons to inaugurate the Taff Trail. 'When he agreed to do it, much to our delight, I did say that it was a rather long ride and offered to shorten it for him, but he was adamant that he would do the whole lot.' Since it was a long ride, though, for several weeks beforehand he went into training, cycling seven or eight miles most evenings.

When he told Tony about what he planned to do, Tony was horrified. 'Geoff, it's likely to be 30 degrees tomorrow, you've had a heart attack and you're seriously thinking of riding 25 miles through the Brecon Beacons?' But Geoff had seen his doctor and had been given the all clear. And once Geoff had made up his mind, there was no changing it.

It was a lovely sunny day, and the town council of Brecon had laid on a reception. Geoff made a speech, and according to Ben Hamilton Baillie, regional director of Sustrans for Wales and the south-west, it was the best speech of the entire summer, encapsulating the whole project better than any other. He spoke about seeing gardening in a wider context, and said that there was no point in doing it unless we took care of the garden of Britain, which belonged to everyone. If we didn't start paying attention to the damage done by the ever-increasing number of cars, then all his work would have been in vain. He said that the Sustrans' initiative had come just in time, and that it was a marvellous way of capturing the public imagination about the larger question of how we can enjoy the countryside without destroying it in the process of getting there. He also unveiled a bronze braille sculpture so that the visually impaired could feel the route. Then, with 200 other cyclists, he set off to cycle the Taff Trail while Lynda drove to meet them at the other end.

Ben Hamilton Baillie cycled with Geoff for an hour or so, chatting happily about the project and plans for a linear garden along the route, and then Sybille Reisen took over. 'Geoff and I were on our own, right at the back, and I think Geoff was finding it quite hard going because he only had a three-speed bike. I did offer to swap bikes with him, but he wouldn't have it. He kept saying to me, "You go ahead. I'll be all right on my own." But I didn't like to leave him. We stopped at the top of the Taff Trail for about 10 minutes and had a drink, and then Geoff got back on his bike and just collapsed.' Sybille immediately cycled off to get help, and a St John's Ambulance nurse tried to resuscitate Geoff on the spot, but it seems that he had died instantly.

Geoff's death was announced on the news that night and in all the papers the next day. The phones in the *Gardeners' World* office didn't stop ringing that week. Many people were in tears, and many of them said it felt as though they had lost a member of their own family. One woman said that as soon as she heard the news, she had decided not to go to work. Instead, she had gone to her local garden centre and bought a shrub, and she was at home now, taking cuttings and potting them up to give to everyone she knew who had loved Geoff, in his memory.

Lynda and the family were inundated with letters of condolence from many people who had met Geoff and also from very many more who hadn't but who felt as if they had, expressing a personal sense of loss. One woman wrote, 'Thank you for lending me Geoff for half an hour every Friday evening. I really feel he's there in my living-room.' A man wrote that Geoff had inspired him to take up horticulture and that his one ambition in life had been to meet him.

Geoff was buried in Exton churchyard in his jeans and boots three days before his sixtieth birthday, Monday 12 August 1996. The tiny church, in the middle of fields, was packed to overflowing with family, friends and colleagues to hear tributes from Tony, Stephen, Nick and Chris. Geoff's grave is in the perfect spot, right in the corner of the churchyard with sheep grazing just a few feet away on the other side of the fence. On it now is planted his favourite tree. A journalist had once asked him what he would like as a memorial, and he had replied, '*Cercidiphyllum japonicum*. It's a lovely honey colour and it will last about 60 years and then die. And that's all right.'

A memorial service – a celebration of the life and skills of Geoff Hamilton – was held in St John's Wood Church, near Lord's Cricket Ground, on 19 December 1996. Again, the church was packed to overflowing, with readings and music – some of Geoff's favourite choral music, like Haydn's *Creation* and Verdi's *Requiem* and, to finish, three rousing jazz numbers from Chris Barber's New Orleans Jazz Band. Some of Geoff's favourite hymns were sung – 'Praise My Soul the King of Heaven', 'God Rest You Merry, Gentlemen' and 'To Be a Pilgrim'.

Alan Titchmarsh spoke warmly about Geoff and read 'Duncton Hill', a poem by one of Geoff's favourite poets, Hilaire Belloc, a lovely and most apposite poem which begins:

> He does not die that can bequeath
> Some influence to the land he knows,
> Or dares, persistent, interwreath
> Love permanent with the wild hedgerows;
> He does not die, but still remains
> Substantiate with his darling plains...

His old friend from rowing days, John Stoddart, read 'The Road of Life' by William Morris, Adam Pasco, editor of *Gardeners' World Magazine*, read from Flora Thompson's *Lark Rise to Candleford*, the managing director of BBC Television, Will Wyatt, read 'The Gardener' by Tagore, and Tony spoke warmly about his brother and his life. It was a wonderfully uplifting service, funny and moving, and everyone said afterwards how much Geoff would have loved it.

In December 1996, Oakham Choral Society dedicated a performance of *Messiah* to Geoff. In the programme, the choirmaster and Head of Academic Music at Oakham School, Peter Witchell, wrote, "This evening's performance is dedicated to the memory of Geoff Hamilton, who joined the society in 1985, for one of his favourite choral pieces, Verdi's *Requiem*. Geoff loved getting away from his busy schedule for a good sing on Monday nights. He was a generous friend to many in the society and a very loyal supporter of everything we have tackled. He enjoyed *Messiah* in particular, and I'm sure he'll be joining us in spirit tonight with his usual boundless enthusiasm, but, much to his pleasure, without on this occasion having to wear a suit.'

Many people wanted to mark Geoff's death in some way, so Lynda nominated Plantlife and Sustrans as charities to which people could make donations in his memory. As a result, not only did Plantlife have enough money to buy the Winskill Stones but there was enough left over to buy Seaton Meadows, the only remaining wetland meadow in Rutland, and not far from Barnsdale, which contained a number of rare species of wild meadow plants. That was dedicated to Geoff's memory by Pippa Greenwood in June 1997 on a lovely warm sunny day. Two weeks later, in starkly contrasting weather conditions, Professor David Bellamy dedicated the Winskill Stones to Geoff's memory.

'There were about a hundred Plantlife members there,' Jane Smart recalls, 'and we all went up on to the towering cliff in driving rain, with a gale howling round us. David Bellamy got up on to a rock and, looking like an Old Testament prophet, addressed the crowd.' He said that 'Geoff was not only a damn good gardener, he was also a good botanist who realized that the plants that gardeners love and cherish all started out as wild flowers, which is why places like the Winskills are so important. With the whole of Britain under threat from changing land use, from the use of chemicals by gardeners and from farming, here was a guy prepared to use his expertise to get conservation across to the mass of Britain's gardeners. We've lost a great campaigner.'

Sustrans is also planning to place a seat on the Taff Trail in Geoff's memory, and the home of organic gardening, the Henry Doubleday Research Association's gardens at Ryton, near Coventry, is planning a paradise garden in Geoff's memory, including many of his favourite plants. That should be open in spring 1999.

Catalyst Television compiled a video for sale with some of the best of Geoff in action. Called *The Barnsdale Collection*, all the profits from it are donated by Catalyst to a charitable trust – Geoff Hamilton New Gardeners' Foundation – to fund scholarships or bursaries for students at his old college, Writtle.

And, of course, Geoff lives on in people's memories. Everywhere the *Gardeners' World* team goes, people always tell us how much they miss him still. And that's because they didn't see him as just a television presenter, quickly forgotten and replaced by a new generation. They really did see him as a friend, someone who was on their side –

an ordinary gardener, just like them. Except, he wasn't ordinary: he was special to millions of people, and especially to those close to him.

In the introduction to this book, Tony has already written very movingly about his feelings for Geoff and the legacy he has left him. His sons miss him terribly too. Chris misses being able to ring him and have long chats on the phone putting the world to rights. And he's also aware of Geoff's legacy to him. 'I've inherited his sense of humour and the fact that if there's a good joke to be made I can't resist making it no matter what price has to be paid. I've also inherited the old man's skinny legs, unfortunately, and also what he used to call "his legs" – a condition where you just can't get your legs to be still or comfortable in bed at night to the point where it keeps you awake. He suffered from it badly, and used to say sometimes, "Terrible legs! In fact I'm starting to get 'legs' in my arms now!"'

Chris has been working on a bust of Geoff in clay, though it will be cast in bronze eventually – an experience that has brought him very close to his father. 'It took me ages to pluck up the courage to start because I had never done a bust before. But once I did start I was up until 4 in the morning, and most of the face came together very quickly. There'd be times when I was patting his cheeks and I'd catch a glimpse of something I'd got right that really was him, and it would startle me – here I was patting my dad's cheeks, and that was something I'd never done when he was alive. It was strange – people often say it must be very odd seeing him on television now. It isn't, but this was. It was deeply moving to be able to create a likeness which was really him. From certain angles it would startle me, and delight me, as if I was with him again.'

Nick, now running Barnsdale Gardens and the nursery, inherited Geoff's love for plants and his work ethic, and he lives with Geoff's memory and presence all the time. 'I know for a fact he's here. You can feel him all over the place, and I do feel in a way that he's directing what I do. And that's very strange because that just isn't me at all. I don't believe in reincarnation or any of that kind of stuff, and yet I do feel very strongly that I'm doing what he wanted.' What Nick misses most is going to the office at the end of the day and having a chat with Geoff. 'It was mostly work-related, but he'd tell me interesting things he'd found out, or funny things, and I'd tell him things that had happened in the day. It's the little things you miss.'

Like Nick, Stephen has inherited Geoff's stubborn gene, along with his love of all the old family stories and sayings, although, as he would be the first to admit, Geoff's work ethic gene has passed him by. 'Geoff was always there to help, and though I fought to stand on my own feet and do my own thing, there was this cocoon of surrounding help. Although I didn't necessarily want or need it, I knew it was there, and now it's gone it does feel very strange.'

Stephen feels, too, that his children have suffered a great loss. 'He used to say to me a lot when I was little, "Oh, it's such a shame that Ally's husband died so young. I'd have loved you to meet him!" and I feel the same about him. He'd have taught my kids all the things he taught me when I was little, and would have thoroughly enjoyed doing it. OK, my two are girls, interested in hair and make-up and the Spice Girls, but he would have got into all that ridiculous nonsense and loved it!'

Lynda sums Geoff up as warm and generous, stubborn and infuriating, loving and lovable. 'He was so caring, and felt he had a duty to look after not only people but every living thing.' For her, the loss is immeasurable, but she wants to do all she can to ensure that his memory lives on and, through it, all the causes that were so important to him, and which, although we may not realize it, are so important to all of us.

Geoff once said, 'The more people I can get to garden, the better the world will be.' On the basis of sheer numbers alone, then, Geoff certainly left the world a better place. But more than that, he enriched all the people whose lives he touched with his true zest for life and for living.

A LAST WORD
FROM TONY HAMILTON

Perhaps we should not think too long or too hard about how Geoff died, but how he lived.

He left behind him, through a short life, a long, long history of love and laughter and goodwill. Geoff was privileged to have more friends than most people even meet – and they all have carefully nurtured memories of his fun, his wisdom and his titanic strength. Nobody who needed a hand up ever left Geoff without some encouragement, some money, some plants, some potatoes, some ideas for their future, or just a feeling that things were going to be OK.

He was tireless in his work, knowing with great certainty that he could help people to discover the joys that he had found in the simple pleasures of a natural way of life. And he was passionate about sending his message to all those who would listen. This was why he worked so hard to hone his presentation skills so that his trusty spade would cut through the hype and glitter of a cruel and self-interested world and reacquaint people with the lost art of living in harmony, with nature and with each other.

He leaves behind a sad family, but a family filled with a quiet pride at their belonging with him. And it is a family that believes in the importance of keeping his memory alive, that the causes he championed live and grow so that his mission remains fresh and fair, and the ordinary people he loved so much can share in the ecstasy he found in his beloved garden.

BIBLIOGRAPHY
OF GEOFF'S BOOKS

'Penny Pinchers' series,
David & Charles 1980:
Growing Soft Fruits; *Herbs and How to
Grow Them*; *Design and Build a Patio or
Terrace*; *Design and Build a Rockery*

Gardeners' World Vegetable Book,
BBC Books 1981

Do Your Own Garden Stonework,
Foulsham 1981

Gardeners' World Cottage Gardens,
BBC Books 1982

The £2 Garden, BBC Books 1983

Gardeners' World Fruit Garden,
BBC Books 1983

Going to Pot, BBC Books 1985

The Budget Garden, BBC Books 1986

Successful Organic Gardening,
Dorling Kindersley 1987

First Time Garden, BBC Books 1988

First Time Planting (with Gay Search),
BBC Books 1989

The Ornamental Kitchen Garden,
BBC Books 1990

Gardeners' World Gardening for Beginners
(with Carol Kurrein), BBC Books 1990

Organic Gardening,
Dorling Kindersley 1991

The Living Garden (with Jennifer
Owen), BBC Books 1992

Old Garden, New Gardener
(with Gay Search), BBC Books 1992

Geoff Hamilton's Gardeners' Challenge
(with Marion and Paddy Lightfoot),
Kingfisher 1993

Gardeners' World Directory,
BBC Books 1993

*Gardeners' World Practical Gardening
Course*, BBC Books 1993

*Gardeners' World Radio Times Gardening
Year* (with Sue Fisher), BBC Books
1994

Geoff Hamilton's Cottage Gardens,
BBC Books 1995

The Complete First Time Gardener
(with Gay Search), BBC Books 1996

Geoff Hamilton's Paradise Gardens,
BBC Books 1997

INDEX